WHITE ELEPHANTS ON CAMPUS

MARGARET M. GRUBIAK

WHITE ELEPHANTS *on* CAMPUS

*The Decline of the University Chapel
in America, 1920–1960*

UNIVERSITY OF NOTRE DAME PRESS
NOTRE DAME, INDIANA

Manufactured in the United States of America

Library of Congress Cataloging-in-Publication Data

Grubiak, Margaret M.
White elephants on campus : the decline of the university chapel in
America, 1920/1960 / Margaret M. Grubiak.
     pages   cm
Includes bibliographical references and index.
ISBN-13: 978-0-268-02987-6 (pbk. : alk. paper)
ISBN-10: 0-268-02987-3 (pbk. : alk. paper)
1. College buildings—United States.   2. Chapels—United States.
3. Church architecture—United States—History—20th century.
4. Education, Higher—Aims and objectives—United States.
5. Education, Higher—United States—History—20th century.
6. Universities and colleges—United States—Religion.   7. Universities
and colleges—United States—History—20th century.   I. Title.
NA6603.G78   2014
726.5097309'04—dc23
                                                        2013044484

For my parents, and for Michael

A world of educated devils is not a pleasant thing to contemplate.

—Reverend Herbert Parrish,
"Religion Goes to College" (1929)

C O N T E N T S

ACKNOWLEDGMENTS

This book, like most, owes a great debt to the great number of people who helped shape and supported it. I would like especially to thank Richard Guy Wilson, Daniel Bluestone, Louis Nelson, and Heather Warren at the University of Virginia. Richard Guy Wilson greatly encouraged this topic and broadened its scope. The incisive criticism of Daniel Bluestone pushed me to consider other perspectives, and Louis Nelson helped immensely in clarifying themes and arguments.

Publication of images in this book was supported by a generous grant from the Graham Foundation for Advanced Studies in the Fine Arts. A grant from the Friends of the Princeton University Library allowed research time at Princeton's Seeley G. Mudd Manuscript Library, and I thank Dan Linke and the library staff for their assistance. Numerous other archives also granted helpful access: Columbia University Archives; University of Chicago Archives; Harvard University Archives; Institute Archives and Special Collections at the Massachusetts Institute of Technology; Manuscripts and Archives at Yale University; the Ferdinand Hamburger Jr. Archives at Johns Hopkins University, especially James Stimpert; University Archives, Illinois Institute of Technology (IIT), especially Catherine Bruck; and University of Pittsburgh Archives, especially Marianne Kasica. I am also grateful to David Sharpe of IIT and Franklin Toker of the University of Pittsburgh for sharing knowledge of their respective campuses.

I thank Villanova University for the generous sabbatical leave to finish this book, my colleagues in the Department of Humanities at Villanova University for their collegiality, and the Office of Scholarly Publications, especially Carole Sargent, at Georgetown University. A Dissertation Year Fellowship from the University of Virginia helped support research for this topic.

I could not have researched this book without the kindness and hospitality of many family and friends, especially Patricia Bennett and Peter Vanderveen in Connecticut; Roysin Bennett Younkin, Jeremy Younkin, and Karen Robbins in Boston; Jeanne McCarthy and Robert Hornback in Washington, DC; and Ron and Pauline Milnarik in Chicago. I am also grateful for the good cheer and encouragement of Paula Mohr and Karen Mulder.

This book is for my very supportive father and mother, Joseph and Mary Anne Grubiak, and my family. My husband, Michael James Tran, showed extraordinary patience and support during the process of research and writing. I am grateful to him for introducing me to many of these universities and for his enthusiasm in exploring architecture wherever we are in the world.

INTRODUCTION

In 1927, nearly six months before the opening of the Princeton University Chapel, the student magazine, the *Princeton Tiger,* published a cartoon that articulated the changing meaning of religious buildings on the American university campus (fig. 0.1). A child stands in front of the chapel asking, "Mummy, *is* that thing a white elephant?"[1] The mother, peering from the edge of the drawing, stares openmouthed at the enormous neo-Gothic facade, offering no response.

The child's question and the mother's silence speak to the transformative shift of religion in the modern American university. In the figure of the child, the cartoon calls into question the significance of the chapel—a seemingly absurd proposition for a brand-new, lavishly constructed religious monument—and suggests the possibility that it is a "white elephant," a euphemism for an expensive but unwanted or useless thing. In the silence of the mother, the cartoon confirms the complexity of the situation. It is not obvious that religion is inconsequential to the university, but it is also not obvious that religion remains central to it. This questioning of whether an enormous, ornate, neo-Gothic chapel was a thing of importance reveals the mutable meaning that college and university chapels came to have by the twentieth century. Whereas religion had a prevalent and assured role in American higher education in the seventeenth, eighteenth, and nineteenth

Figure 0.1. A 1927 *Princeton Tiger* cartoon depicting the Princeton University Chapel and the question, "Mummy, *is* that thing a white elephant?" From *Princeton Tiger* 37, no. 7 (15 December 1927): 34, Princeton University Archives, Department of Rare Books and Special Collections, Princeton University Library.

centuries, by the interwar decades of the twentieth century religion's role was precarious and changing.

The mother and child also represent a significant generational divide in the perception of religion in the university in the early twentieth century. For many coming of age in the 1920s and 1930s, like the inquisitive child, the sense that religion's role in higher education had declined was palpable and even welcomed. Student-led campaigns had largely ended mandatory chapel policies—the requirement that students attend daily or weekly religious services—by the 1920s. The influx of students from a variety of backgrounds also challenged Protestant hegemony in American universities. Science, too, claimed a dominant voice in the university, offering new, and presumably better, ways to verifiable knowledge. For this generation and those that followed, university education did not need to include a religious education. In fact, to do so would make a university less modern and less progressive.

But for many university presidents, like the responsible adult in the cartoon, the possibility that religion no longer had a significant role in higher education was an unsettling sea change. University leaders still believed it was the duty of the university to educate moral citizens, even amidst an increasingly secularized American culture. They were loath to give up the idea of religion and morality in the project of higher education. Their backing of university chapel construction confirms their continued desire to see religion as a part of higher education. These university leaders employed a number of ways to inscribe religion in the physical campus, including using architecture to advance a religious identity. Yet even such attempts could not prevent the emerging view of religious buildings as white elephants.

The questioning of the Princeton University Chapel as a white elephant is a stunning example of how architecture manifested the changing role of religion in American higher education. This book examines the shifting meaning of religious architecture on the American university campus from the 1920s to the 1960s. It looks specifically at elite Protestant universities that had the choice of continuing a religious identity or negotiating a new relationship with religion in the modern era. It argues that college and university chapels, and other religious-like buildings on campus, attempted to broker a new role for religion. Although we now associate university chapels (when we actually think of them) with alumni weddings and the occasional service, in the early twentieth century these buildings were embroiled in a debate over religion's place in higher education. The religious landscape in the physical campus records this struggle and the ultimate inability to keep religion as a core component of the university mission. By the 1960s, university chapels had indeed become white elephants on campus relative to the principal aim of higher education.

THE AMERICAN UNIVERSITY
AND THE SECULARIZATION THESIS

The idea that American colleges moved from a focus on religious education—primarily intended for the training of ministers—to universities focused on science and the production of empirical truth is part of the much-debated secularization thesis. This thesis proposes that as societies become more technologically and socially advanced, religion becomes less influential, until eventually widespread secularism takes hold.[2] In the history of higher education in the United States, the removal of religion from a place of authority is particularly striking. Protestant interests had long controlled the American academy, in some cases for centuries, but by the mid- to late twentieth century conceptions of American higher education for nondenominational schools had almost nothing to do with religion. As the historians George Marsden, Julie Rueben, Douglas Sloan, Jon Roberts, and James Turner have contended, the advent of science, changing notions of truth, and even efforts by Protestants themselves gradually undermined the authority of religion in the academy.[3] Recent scholarship has tempered the conception of the wholesale removal of religion from the university, rightfully arguing that the practice of religion remains vibrant in some university communities and has been resurgent in the past decade.[4] However, the broad trend of universities turning away from their religious foundations remains a convincing part of American higher education's historical narrative, and the physical landscape of the campus bears out this transformation.

By the 1920s, religion in the university was markedly changed. Older institutions had once been tied to and supported by particular denominations. But by the late nineteenth century, historically Congregationalist Yale and Anglican King's College (later Columbia University), for example, were no longer under the control of these Protestant denominations, though they retained their Christian character vocally.[5] Newly founded universities made firm pledges of nonsectarianism. At its opening in 1876, Johns Hopkins University claimed no particular denominational affiliation, and although the University of Chicago grew out of Baptist support, in the 1890s it also proclaimed itself nonsectarian but Christian. Many universities removed the professions of faith requirement for professors and presidents. With the growth in the student population, the university no longer had a religiously homogeneous student body, making the assertion of one religious perspective problematic.

To skirt emerging theological divides, emphasis within the university shifted to a more generic religiosity and a focus on character. As James Burtchaell argues, calls to pietism in university education still reigned strong, but such calls were superficial. The promotion of good character had replaced dogmatic religion, and religion itself had become "only one element in the Whole Man, who was now understood as a paladin of civic virtues."[6] George Marsden argues that because Protestants now located Christianity "in individual experiences and in public morality," "distinctive Christian theological principles" could not be maintained in universities that did not fashion themselves as specifically denominational institutions.[7] Only a vague appeal to character and morality could.

The fervent belief that science was the path to a new, definite truth contributed to the decline of religion's authority within the university's intellectual life. With methods that produced verifiable and (supposedly) unbiased results, science held the promise of uncovering an unwavering truth. Initially scientific investigation was united with religion in purpose. Natural theology, which dominated scientific inquiry in the nineteenth century, provided an apology for religion by ascribing natural phenomena to God's grand design. Victorian beliefs easily aligned religion, science, and social reform. But as science became specialized, such a vague and large-scale conclusion as "God is the reason" grew unsatisfying.[8] The search for more specific answers, along with an emphasis on objectivity, distanced faith from the scientific process. As quantitative, objective ways of knowing were privileged, the academic community marginalized truths of "faith, religious experience, morality, meaning and value" precisely because they were not grounded "in accepted, potentially knowable reality."[9] Scientific inquiry "by its very nature undermined the status of the kind of belief, trust, and commitment that lay at the heart of religious faith."[10] By the early twentieth century, scientists replaced clerics in a "new order of sainthood" within the university.[11]

Proponents of religion in the academy paradoxically aided this secularization process. Sloan suggests that churches themselves saw the progression of higher education as the purveyor of scientific knowledge as evidence of the arrival of the kingdom of God and of natural progress in civilization.[12] Marsden argues that the steps toward secularization were in fact benign. Even those of devout faith distanced religion from science in order to better the scientific process. Liberal Protestants, though attempting to reconcile religion and science, paved the way for secularization because they believed so strongly that science could offer a definite morality. This belief that science and religion were aligned lessened in some ways the anxiety about changes in the university's priorities. Many university presidents and leaders optimistically believed that science and religion could be real partners in the modern university—an optimism that would be greatly challenged.

The American university in the interwar decades was an institution caught within this new landscape of an increasingly scientific culture. Those who believed that the university had a responsibility to attend to a religious and particularly Christian formation of their students sensed this threat. Their attempts to counter it created a university campus in which religion was both overtly and subtly inscribed.

RELIGION ON CAMPUS

While religious historians have acknowledged the importance of architecture in the changing place of religion in the university—an image of the Stanford University Memorial Church (1898–1903) serves as the frontispiece of George Marsden's *The Soul of the American University*—this book takes an architectural history approach to understand what the material campus reveals about the role of religion in the university in a forty-year period, from the 1920s to the 1960s.

This book is not an exhaustive survey of campus chapels in the United States. I have excluded chapels at denominational institutions as the natural expectation of religious buildings on these campuses masked the ambiguities about religion in the university that I am attempting to uncover. Similarly, I do not examine chapels on public campuses as respect for the separation of church and state often—but not always—led to the exclusion of religious buildings there.[13] Rather, I focus on elite universities, most with a Protestant heritage, including Harvard University, Johns Hopkins University, Princeton University, Yale University, and the Massachusetts Institute of Technology. These universities ostensibly had a choice, without denominational pressure or legal restrictions, of whether and how to reframe their relationship with religion. What this book seeks to do is uncover broad themes of how the religious image was transformed and ultimately marginalized in the American university.

Chapter 1 explores the challenges to religion on campus, including the increasing dominance of science as the valued system of truth and the growing movement against compulsory worship services. It also details the ways university leaders still believed in the project of religion, especially through the lens of the "whole man" theory of education and the liberal Protestant hope for the reconciliation of science and religion. These leaders believed that the physical expression of religion on the campus could stem the tide of secularization and even spark a renewed religious commitment.

Architecture was fundamental to the attempt to retain religion in the university in four principal ways. First, chapels in the early twentieth century became ways to advertise religion's enduring significance to the university, the focus of chapter 2. In the 1920s, advocates for a new, larger church on Harvard Yard claimed that the university "advertises" in the very size of the building the number of people it expected to attend services.[14] The size of these chapels was indeed crucial to suggesting religion's continued influence. A 1929 book on collegiate architecture described the neo-Gothic chapels at the University of Chicago and Princeton University, both seating about two thousand worshippers, as "the most ambitious university chapels ever seen in this country," just as those universities loosened their policies on required attendance at worship services.[15] Paradoxically, as religion's influence on the intellectual life and daily practice on campus was waning, religion's architectural image on campus was at its strongest.

Chapter 2 also takes up a second method university leaders employed to retain religion's relevance: the emotional appeal to religious worship, even if this went against Protestant tenets. In the 1920s, the architect Ralph Adams Cram with his partner, Frank Ferguson, based the design of Princeton University Chapel on pre-Reformation Gothic architecture. Their neo-Catholic cathedral drew its power from an evocation of emotion, from the traditional stained glass to the high, vaulted ceiling to the associated ritual—far from the austere Protestant meeting-houses focused on the spoken word. The chapel's design infuriated those who located Protestantism within an appeal to the intellect rather than the senses, and yet for Princeton students the emotional appeal proved effective. While it is true that the choice to build chapels in the collegiate Gothic style also played on nonreligious associations with Britain's Oxford and Cambridge Universities, many traditionally Protestant universities turned again and again to the Gothic-Catholic imagery in spite of the theological dissonance in order to draw students back to worship.

A third strategy was to place religion at the center of campus, the focus of chapter 3. Campus plans, influenced by Beaux Arts axiality, put a special emphasis on the center, the logical location of the buildings with the greatest symbolic meaning to the mission of the university. Many campus plans in the interwar decades juxtaposed the chapel and the library at the center to articulate religion and learning as the key components of higher education. While this was the ideal, in practice religion often failed to find its way to the campus core. Chapter 3 takes up the planning of Johns Hopkins University, Harvard University, and Yale University in their struggle—sometimes successful, sometimes not—to place religion at the center of the modern campus.

In a fourth strategy to keep religion relevant to the academic work at hand, university leaders and architects imbued nonreligious structures with religious meaning. Although the University of Pittsburgh constructed a traditional chapel on its campus, the building that more strongly symbolized religion was the forty-two-story Cathedral of Learning skyscraper classroom. When the architect James Gamble Rogers's proposed five-thousand-seat chapel for the Yale center was not realized, his Sterling Memorial Library became the university's cathedral-library, reinterpreting religion at the heart of campus. The entrance hall of the library was a nave space with the card catalog placed in the side aisles. The confessionals in the narthex hosted the telephone booths. Visitors checked out books at the circulation desk-cum-altar under the guise of the *Alma Mater* altarpiece, whose figure made a direct allusion to the Virgin Mary. Chapter 4 examines the Cathedral of Learning and the Sterling Memorial Library in detail in their ecclesiastical metaphors, arguing that religion was transformed as a background to the work of the modern university. Yet this strategy created multiple interpretations, including the mockery of religion. The ecclesiastical metaphor proved a double-edged sword.

These interwar examples were the height of the attempts to retain a strong architectural and visual presence of religion on campus. Following World War II, religion on the university and college campus looked markedly different, thanks in large part to the influence of modernism. But stylistic choice was not the only major distinguishing factor. A new sensitivity to other faith traditions also inspired a new era of ecumenical worship spaces. Chapter 5 examines one significant postwar example, Eero Saarinen's Massachusetts Institute of Technology Chapel, which recrafted a New England meetinghouse on the common and used non-specific religious symbols to create a worship space that would accommodate Protestant, Catholic, and Jewish services. Importantly, Saarinen's chapel also speaks to a significant shift in size. While MIT wanted to construct a chapel to remind its students of the responsibility of science to society following the dropping of the atomic bomb, the university did not see religion as a common, large-scale community exercise. The chapel seats only about seventy-five worshippers, exemplary of the postwar trend toward smaller university chapels. On campus in the 1950s, religion was transformed into a largely individual, voluntary, meditative, and nondenominational event. Religion was present within higher education but no longer held a central role.

The 1960s brought even greater changes on the university campus, with religion even more marginalized. Chapel building on nondenominational campuses slowed, and energies shifted to the construction of separate buildings for individual religious denominations—Catholic Newman Centers, Methodist Wesley Centers, Episcopalian Canterbury Fellowship Centers, and Jewish Hillels—on the campus periphery, whose architectural, cultural, and religious history remains to be written. For many American universities, the dominant image of religion on campus remains that crafted in the first half of the twentieth century. While these chapels were constructed with great optimism, over time the conception of the chapels and other religious-like buildings has become transformed. They remain beautiful structures, important to those who begin their married lives there, to those who find solace in meditation and prayer within their walls, and to those who in the midst of commencement ceremonies contemplate their futures. But they are no longer a place central to the university mission or identity. They are now white elephants.

CHAPTER I

THE CHAPEL
IN THE AGE OF
SCIENCE

A remarkable experiment performed in St. Paul's Chapel at Columbia University in 1908 made visible one of most important questions troubling the modern American university: What was the place of religion in an academic environment increasingly dominated by scientific ideals? Framed against three stained-glass panels in the chancel of Saint Paul preaching to the Athenians by the noted American artist John LaFarge, the thin steel thread of a pendulum anchored by a two-hundred-pound shell hung from the chapel's nine-story dome (fig. 1.1). The pendulum, named for its inventor, the nineteenth-century French physicist Jean-Bernard-Léon Foucault, demonstrated the earth's rotation as gravitational pull shifted the pendulum's course from a straight line to an elliptical swing. Once put in motion, Foucault's pendulum traced the outline of an ellipse in the chapel's central aisle. Nearly two thousand students and visitors came to St. Paul's Chapel to witness this scientific spectacle.[1]

Foucault's pendulum represented the power of science to explain the world. Science provided concrete, repeatable, verifiable knowledge

Figure 1.1. Foucault's pendulum experiment performed in St. Paul's Chapel, Columbia University, 1908. From "The Foucault's Pendulum in St. Paul's Chapel," *Columbia University Quarterly* (March 1908): 194. Courtesy of University Archives, Columbia University in the City of New York.

that had special and growing importance within the university. As American universities shifted their mission away from the training of ministers and toward knowledge production, empirical knowledge garnered increasing authority and value over revealed, or religious, knowledge. This shift is what made the display of Foucault's pendulum so arresting. The experiment in the chapel made material the changing and as yet unresolved relationship between science and religion in the modern American university, powerfully suggesting the ways in which religion and science could work together while simultaneously visualizing the possibility and even reality of science overtaking religion in the university's mission.

For some visitors to the exhibition, the threat of science to religion was very real. In a letter of protest to the president of Columbia University over the display of the pendulum in the chapel, one alumnus and trustee named John Pine declared "that the Chapel should not be used for any purpose whatever, however proper in itself, which is in the least degree inconsistent with the religious character of the building."[2] Underlying Pine's protest was the anxiety that science was indeed replacing religion, not only as a dominant system of knowledge, but also as a dominant area of interest and practice in the university. Furthermore, for Pine, science violated the sacredness of the chapel itself. Secular knowledge, his protest implied, was separate from divine knowledge, and each required a separate environment for its understanding and practice. Religion in this view needed to be protected from the encroachment of science. While Pine may have granted the significance and veracity of science in itself, he sought to preserve the significance and sanctity of religion in the university.

For Columbia University president Nicholas Murray Butler, that such an experiment should be conducted in the chapel was far from problematic. Butler's response to Pine unified science and religion in the modern university. Butler argued that Focault's pendulum, which he deemed "one of the most impressive experiments known to modern science," was in fact "a rather exceptionally appropriate use of the Chapel." Scientific experimentation and religious worship simultaneously inhabiting the same space moved toward the same end. Witnessing the experiment generated "feelings of awe," Butler claimed, which "associate themselves naturally enough with a religious building."[3]

Butler's answer brilliantly aligned science with religion. In characterizing the outcomes of science as awe inducing, he claimed that every search for truth, even by scientific means, was fundamentally religious in nature, leading to a fuller understanding of a world created by God. From this perspective, science, far from a godless pursuit meant to disprove the tenets of religion, in fact gave evidence of the divine. Such a view allowed the unfettered practice of science and yet preserved the enduring significance of religion. This rationale, rooted in the liberal Protestant tradition, was one used again and again by university presidents and leaders well into the twentieth century as a way to reconcile the American university as a vanguard in knowledge production and yet an institution still beholden to the moral formation of its students.

Of course, Butler's view of the cooperation between science and religion was an optimistic one. Understood another way, this alliance put religion in the background of modern scientific work and in danger of being superseded by it. By the 1960s, religion was indeed relegated to the peripheral concerns of the university due, in part, to this earlier formulation of religion's role. But in the early twentieth century, marrying science and religion to the idea of understanding God's greatness in the world was deemed the best route to negotiating a new place for religion in the university. The display of Foucault's pendulum in a university chapel spoke to the important role that religious architecture on campus was to play in this negotiation.

CHALLENGES TO RELIGION IN THE MODERN AMERICAN UNIVERSITY

John Pine's concern over the threat to religion in the university had a real foundation. The modern American university of the late nineteenth and early twentieth century had become something much different from the college of antebellum America.[4] In the antebellum college, religion was the central, authoritative, and cohesive force. Early American colleges were largely founded by Protestant denominations with a primary mission to educate and train clergy. Columbia University (originally King's College) was Anglican; Yale, Congregationalist; Brown, Baptist; and Princeton (originally the College of New Jersey), closely aligned with the Presbyterian Church. These denominations gave financial support to these colleges and governed their administration, rules and practices, mission, and course content. Clergy were often college presidents and assumed other leadership positions. Students were required to attend regular religious services (as was true of many early public colleges) and adhere to strict codes of conduct. The college curriculum emphasized the classical texts, and theology was also a curriculum component. In the early American college, religion held a pervasive and primary role.

Yet following the Civil War, the central role of religion shifted as a reform movement reshaped the American college into the more intellectually rigorous and progressive American university. Pivotal to this transformation was the influence of the German university model. In the second half of the nineteenth century, Americans studying at German universities returned to the United States imbued with the German ideal of pure research—the search for knowledge simply for knowledge's sake—as well as increased standards for scientific research, a focus on faculty scholarship, the importance of graduate education and professional schools, and a model of academic freedom, including the elective system. Although universities in the United States transformed these ideals for their own ends, the German model formed the basis for the modern American university, which privileged the pursuit of verifiable truth over other aspects of education.[5]

The emphasis on research and empirical methods of inquiry displaced religion from the center of the university's intellectual life. To pursue research to its own ends, scientists and others needed academic freedom to examine empirical evidence unencumbered, without the strictures of religious doctrine and belief. American universities took steps to ensure that freedom. By the late nineteenth and early twentieth century, private American universities had largely cut ties with their founding religious denominations, meaning that financial control, oversight of the faculty, and determination of the curriculum were no longer under the watchful eye of the church. The Carnegie

Foundation encouraged the distancing of universities from their religious foundations as a method of institutional reform, requiring in 1905 that universities renounce their denominational ties in order to receive pension support for their faculty.[6] The transformation to the modern American university seemed to require a lesser role for religion.

Religion was becoming displaced from the university's intellectual life in other ways. With the PhD a growing prerequisite for teaching, the university professoriate became the purview not of clergy but of highly trained academics. And whereas the American college had focused strongly on the moral, spiritual, social, and intellectual development of undergraduates, in which religion had played a central part, the modern American university gave greater emphasis to graduate education. In the classroom, theology was substituted with morality and secular humanism, leading William F. Buckley Jr. to claim in the 1950s in *God and Man at Yale* that religion was no longer part of the curriculum and that students' religious beliefs had been marginalized in the classroom.[7] While scholars have appropriately argued the need for nuance in understanding exactly to what extent religion was relegated to the margins of the university's intellectual life, the fact remains that religion's sway in the modern American university was transformed by a new culture dominated by research and science.

WANING WORSHIP ON CAMPUS

Just as the place of religion was changing in the university's intellectual life, so too was the landscape of religious worship on campus. Required daily or weekly worship had been a traditional component of the American college and had driven chapel building on American campuses. Corporate worship served the mission of the university in several respects. First, it reinforced the Christian, though nonsectarian, identity and aims with which many colleges and universities still associated. Second, compulsory chapel brought students together for regular worship services that not only inculcated religious teachings on an individual level but also fostered a sense of and duty to community. But by the late nineteenth century, the mandatory chapel requirement came under attack. Dissatisfied with the poor quality of the services and the chapel buildings themselves, resentful of being compelled to worship, and fed up with getting out of bed early, many students challenged the value of mandatory chapel in the formation of religious belief.

By many accounts, mandatory services had become dismal events. At daily chapel at Yale University in the late nineteenth century, a tradition since the school's founding in 1701, students arrived at chapel ten to fifteen minutes late, some only half dressed, with overcoats over their pajamas. Some read the newspaper and completed their homework during the service.[8] At Princeton's mandatory chapel services, newspaper reading also commonly occurred, and long services and prayers were met with protests of coughing fits.[9] A 1905 cartoon in the *Princeton Tiger* lampooned the intimation that one could earn a halo simply by collecting "chapel checks" that proved attendance (fig. 1.2).[10] Compulsory chapel implied that students became religious by passively attending worship services irrespective of their real belief, sincerity, or participation. In 1926, Frank Butterworth, Yale alumnus and football hero, wrote in a petition to end Yale's compulsory chapel, "Our chapel has lost too much of its atmosphere of a church. Its pulpit has been occupied too frequently by some one who takes his turn at a chore of that day and inspires no reverence. Its service has become too unimpressive and ordinary to be defended or to be a beneficial religious occasion. There it ought not to be." More pointedly, he opined, "The system of compulsory chapel is tending to do more harm to religion than good. Our chapel is more a mockery of a religious atmosphere and service than a reality, and so hurts."[11] Furthermore, the increasing religious plurality of the student body diminished the significant religious content of the services. The former chairman of the *Yale Daily News* argued that the services had lost most of their meaning in an effort to not be offensive to any religion.[12]

The arguments made against compulsory chapel by students, alumni, and some faculty proved effective. Harvard was the first to end its compulsory services in 1886. Yale followed forty years later, in 1926. At about the same time, the University of Chicago dropped the compulsory chapel requirement, just eighteen months before the completion of its immense, 2,500-seat chapel in 1928.[13] Though students still

Figure 1.2. A 1905 *Princeton Tiger* cartoon satirizing mandatory chapel and the exchange of "chapel checks" for holiness. From *Princeton Tiger* 16, no. 2 (October 1905), Princeton University Archives, Department of Rare Books and Special Collections, Princeton University Library.

attended regular Sunday services at the Princeton University Chapel's opening in 1928, seven years later, in 1935, this requirement no longer applied to upperclassmen. While smaller services continued on campus, by the outbreak of World War II widespread corporate worship in most major American universities no longer existed.

PRESERVING RELIGION:
THE "WHOLE MAN" THEORY
AND THE LIBERAL PROTESTANT SYNTHESIS

These changes within the modern American university—the adherence to a new code of research and specialization and the marginalization of religion in university life—sparked a backlash. Many university leaders still believed in religion's project to shape moral people and good citizens. They saw adherence to the German model as a threat to the long-standing mission of higher education. The writings of Ralph Adams Cram, a prolific author, campus planner, and architect, are exemplary of the criticism of this German model of higher education and vividly distilled the ways in which it had changed American higher education from a classically liberal education to knowledge production. From Cram's perspective, the German influence had corrupted education, introduced secularism, denied the importance of religion, and reduced education to the mere acquisition of skills for income-producing jobs. He decried the notion that the "object of education" had turned into, "not the building of character, but the breeding of intensive specialists, or the turning of a boy at the earliest possible moment into a wage earning animal." Cram bitingly captured the ill effects of adherence to the German model of education:

> It is not so long ago that our ideal seemed to be a kind of so-called education that might be labeled "Made in Germany": we prescribed nothing, and accepted anything a freshman in his wisdom might elect; we joined schools of dental surgery and "business science," whatever that may be, and journalism and farriery [blacksmithing] to our august universities; we ignored Greek and smiled at Latin; we tried to

teach theology on an undogmatic basis, an idea not without humor; and we cut out religious worship altogether.[14]

Cram and others who believed in the higher purposes of education found the corrective to this perceived corruption in the British "whole man" theory of education. This theory returned the focus to the undergraduate and sought to cultivate students' entire development—intellectual, moral, spiritual, and social. Subscribers to the theory found its exemplar at Oxford and Cambridge. The Oxbridge educational system seemed to produce the ideal gentleman student, possessed with a sound liberal education, widely read, and well mannered. American educators took Oxbridge as their literal model, building residential quadrangles in an appropriation of the English educational model. Harvard's undergraduate houses and Yale's colleges, constructed largely in the 1920s and 1930s, were a direct emulation of the Oxbridge ideal of placing students in close proximity to their teachers. Within these quadrangles students dined in common, played in common, and lived in communion with a faculty master. Such environments humanized the educational experience in the midst of specialization and scientific production, promoted esprit de corps among the growing university population, and preserved and even heightened the sense of academic tradition within the newness of the university identity. In replicating Oxbridge, presidents found ways to cope with the dramatically evolving nature of the American university. While the modern American university persisted in following the German model with an emphasis on research and graduate education, the countervailing whole man theory, based on the British model, sought to hold onto traditional ideals in undergraduate education that privileged the development of character and morality.[15]

The whole man theory promoted the shaping of students into moral, responsible citizens willing to serve causes larger than themselves. University leaders believed that it was the responsibility of the university to produce graduates who would become the next leaders and stewards of the greater community, as Princeton University president Woodrow Wilson affirmed in the 1890s with his famous emphasis on service to the nation. Promoting moral and religious values was a way to instill this sense of selflessness and community service. Moreover, scientific advances called for morally and religiously conscious graduates who would use new knowledge in a responsible manner, as the dramatic end of World War II underscored. As Cram claimed, "We have pretty well learned by this time that there is no effective education that is not interpenetrated by religion at every point."[16]

Proponents of the whole man theory often overlapped with the liberal Protestant view of the alliance of science and religion in the university. Modern American university leaders did not wish to deny science's value to university work. Empirical research, adherence to the scientific method, and academic freedom had raised the status of the university and moved it into new, fruitful paths. And yet these leaders were also loath to embrace the idea that religion and the development of the moral student were no longer part of higher education's mission. Liberal Protestantism provided a path that could hold religion alongside science in the university mission. This explains why Butler at Columbia University, himself an adherent of liberal Protestantism, could optimistically proclaim that the Foucault's pendulum experiment produced the same effect as a religious experience. Liberal Protestants asserted that scientific discoveries were at root religious in nature, irrespective of the challenges, such as Darwin's theory of evolution, posed to religious tradition, because such discoveries revealed God's immanence or presence in the world.[17] In fact, liberal Protestants had great enthusiasm for science. They believed that by unlocking key principles science would lead to a higher, universal morality.[18] In recognizing, accepting, and even promoting science's importance, liberal Protestants maintained a Christian perspective within the scientific intellectual climate of the American university.

In arguing for a new chapel for Yale University in the 1920s, Chaplain Elmore McKee put forward a classic liberal Protestant argument that every search for truth in the university, including empirical investigation, was a form of worship. He claimed that "every legitimate phase of a university's life, if pursued to its deeper levels, leads to worship." For McKee, "the astronomer at his telescope, or the biologist at his microscope, is asking the question, 'Is there a purpose in the universe and in life, which links together the stars or water-life and the personality making the investigation?'" This search for knowledge was fundamentally tied to a religious experience: "Now the instant a man is conscious of his search for an Order, a Plan, a Purpose beyond himself, he is at the threshold of worship."[19] In framing all pursuits of truth against the background of revealing a larger purpose, liberal Protestants found a way to keep religion part of the university project and mission, important not only as the ultimate reason in intellectual pursuits but also to the formation of character and morality in the student. In the interwar decades, the liberal Protestant reconciliation of science and religion was pivotal in the attempt to forge an enduring role for religion in modern intellectual life.

THE ARCHITECTURAL ARGUMENT FOR RELIGION

Religious buildings on the American university campus visualized the coordinated attempt to preserve religion within a changing intellectual and cultural landscape. Columbia University president Butler pointed to St. Paul's Chapel as evidence of the desire "to spare no effort to give religious influence, religious aspiration and religious service their appropriate place in the life of a great company of students who are spending years precious for the formation of mind and character in residence at the University."[20] Princeton University president John Grier Hibben would not entertain proposals to end mandatory chapel entirely until after the new Princeton University Chapel was constructed, ensuring the prominent presence of religion on the campus.[21] These university leaders saw religion as having an enduring role in the academy. University chapels and other buildings that appropriated religious imagery mediated the relationship between religion and the emerging scientific culture on the university campus in architectural terms. Though science increasingly occupied the workaday life of the university, it did so in buildings that comprised the substance of the campus but not its symbolic core. The chapel building itself, often prominently situated at the campus center, promoted the relationship between science and religion and between modernity and tradition.

Perceptions of that relationship, however, varied. To those who drove their construction, namely, university presidents, alumni, and patrons, many of whom were liberal Protestants and proponents of the whole man theory of higher education, university chapels were adamant statements that religion would remain a crucial part of university life even as empirical knowledge grew in stature. The chapels were to remind students of the ultimate purpose of learning; they were to be didactic tools in promoting Christianity; and they were to proclaim the respectful, complementary coexistence of science and religion. Yet to others, they were perplexing monuments of a Protestant culture caught in watershed change. To still others, they were white elephants of a tradition already surpassed by a secular, scientific worldview. As George Marsden has claimed, the chapels arising on the modern university campus were "monuments to a disappearing Christian ideal."[22] Though these large, extravagant chapels were optimistic proclamations of religion's continuing importance on the campus prima facie, they also reflected the changing place of religion within the milieu of the modern university.

CHAPTER 2

THE IMAGE
OF UNIVERSITY
RELIGION

University chapels constructed in the interwar decades of the twentieth century embodied a paradox: Just as attacks on mandatory chapel services were at their peak and the role of religion in the university mission was shifting, the architectural image of religion on campus was at its strongest. Lavish, large-scale chapel buildings projected a sense of strength, vitality, and permanence and conspicuously displayed the immense resources devoted to the project of religion on campus. This robust religious image in the face of shifting university priorities was no accident. University presidents, leaders, and donors enlisted architecture to argue that religion should and must retain its vital place in the formation of the whole student. They believed that an emotional appeal to religion could entice students back to worship, and they often turned to neo-Gothic forms to create sensuous worship environments irrespective of Protestant traditions. The university chapel in the interwar decades, through its lavish image, became a polemical tool to advertise, affirm, and revive religion's role in American higher education.

THE CHAPEL AS ADVERTISEMENT

At more than any other point in the history of American higher education, the chapels constructed on campus in the early twentieth century advertised the importance of religion to the university mission in their very presence and size. The conception of the chapel as advertisement became critical to the modern American university facing increasing challenges to mandatory worship. The construction of chapel buildings among new university equipment was used to refute the contention that religion's influence on campus was waning. Princeton trustee Edward Duffield claimed that the construction of the new Princeton University Chapel in the 1920s affirmed the university's commitment to religion even "when funds are still inadequate, when religious controversy is raging, when required Sunday Chapel is being attacked."[1] In 1930, the journal *Christian Education*, a publication of the Council of Church Boards of Education (later renamed the National Protestant Council on Higher Education), argued vigorously against the suggestion that student protests against compulsory chapel were a sign that "the college chapel as an agency of religious culture is obsolescent if not obsolete." The journal published pictures and descriptions of some thirty-nine college and university chapels in the United States, most of them recently constructed or planned, as evidence of a "renaissance rather than a retrogression" of the influence of the chapel in sustaining religious life.[2] The chapel building itself became an advertisement to proclaim the health of religion in the university even as undercurrents challenged this image of strength and vitality.

The very presence of a chapel building on campus conveyed the university's position on the role of religion. From the 1890s into the 1930s, construction on university campuses reached unprecedented proportions as well-established institutions like Harvard, Yale, and Princeton invested millions in new buildings to shape a university identity apart from their collegiate foundations and as new institutions like Stanford University and the University of Chicago created campuses de novo. Having resources dedicated to the construction of chapel buildings was an important signifier of the university's values. A new chapel among the new laboratories, libraries, lecture halls, and dormitories signaled the university's commitment to religion even as it accommodated the needs of research and science. Conversely, the lack of a chapel seemed to suggest a negative posture on religion, even if this was not the university's stated position. One Yale University alumnus asserted that the fact Yale had not built a new, larger chapel as part of its extensive building campaign in the 1920s was evidence to the average undergraduate "of a steadily waning importance of the spiritual side of life in the estimation of the governing and teaching authorities of the University."[3] By allowing the Victorian Battell Chapel and the antebellum Dwight Hall, renovated to include a small chapel, to be the enduring images of religion, the Yale campus communicated that traditional religion had been left behind in the nineteenth century, while the new residential quadrangles, graduate schools, and research library—even though themselves rendered in a historicist architectural vocabulary—assumed the focus of the modern university. Although Yale's administration under President James Rowland Angell was in fact supportive of religion, the campus itself communicated a contradictory message.

The immense scale of university chapels also advanced the idea of religion as remaining a central part of the university mission. The chapels rising on university campuses in the early twentieth century were quite simply enormous. In their 1929 book on collegiate architecture, the architects Charles Z. Klauder and Herbert C. Wise described the recently completed neo-Gothic chapels at the University of Chicago and Princeton University as "the most ambitious university chapels ever seen in this country."[4] The Princeton University and University of Chicago chapels each accommodated over two thousand worshippers. The chapel James Gamble Rogers proposed for Yale in the 1920s was to seat an astonishing five thousand, which would have been the largest university chapel in the world. These chapels vied for contention among the largest university buildings. Of the buildings constructed between 1893 and 1932 at the University of Chicago, the Rockefeller Memorial Chapel (1928) nearly matched the size of the Harper Memorial Library and was only clearly overshadowed in size by the expansive medical campus.[5] The financial and spatial resources dedicated to these chapel buildings signified the desire that religion remain a critical part of the university mission, even and especially as the long-standing tradition of compulsory chapel came to an end. If university leaders could not stem the tide against mandatory chapel attendance, they could control the physical and visual expressions of religion on the campus.

The interplay of chapel presence, newness, and large scale in asserting religion's relevance within the modern university was central to the debate over a new church at Harvard University in the 1920s and 1930s. Advocates of a new chapel building argued that the size of the chapel advertised the importance of religion to the university. A 1925 report to the Board of Overseers of Harvard College noted that about one-third of the time the Sunday attendance at Harvard's 1853 Appleton Chapel exceeded its 870-seat capacity.[6] The Board of College Preachers argued that the "University advertises by the size of this chapel" the number it expected to attend worship and that the chapel's smaller size limited "its invitation to the number it can accommodate." "The student estimates values by the standards before him," the report claimed. "As things are the average student is forced to the conclusion that there is no great desire on the part of the University that he should attend Sunday worship at the University chapel."[7]

For Harvard, a new, larger chapel was a statement that religion could be successful even with voluntary chapel policies. Harvard had been the first major institution of higher education to end its mandatory chapel policy in 1886. Professor Edward Caldwell Moore, former president of the Board of College Preachers, believed that Harvard, as the "inaugurators" and "still the most conspicuous exponents of the system of voluntary attendance and interdenominational administration," needed to set an example for those colleges and universities then engaged in the compulsory chapel debate. "It would be a pity," he wrote, "if those who are now perplexed should infer from our mere failure to follow up our success that we ourselves do not feel sure that we have taken the right course for religion in the educational world."[8] A new and immense chapel would prove that the switch to voluntary worship had not harmed Harvard's religious life. Irrespective of the actual numbers of those who attended, the scale of the chapel would advertise the success of voluntary chapel at Harvard and counter its reputation for being "godless." Despite some protests from alumni saying religion on campus had in fact declined and therefore a new chapel was unnecessary, a new and larger chapel was constructed in Harvard Yard. With room for twelve hundred worshippers—nearly four hundred more than the previous chapel—and a soaring spire, the new Harvard Memorial Church, dedicated in 1931, sent a strong message about the health of religion at Harvard in the interwar decades.

APPEALING TO THE EMOTIONS AT PRINCETON

If one strategy to affirm religion's role in the university was to build large-scale chapels, another was to construct worship spaces that appealed to the emotions. Architecture's sensual experience presented a powerful means to newly reengage students in religious worship. The alignment of religion with emotion also cast religion against science's cold rationalism. Among those who believed that religion's emotional appeal was the best and perhaps only way to save religion on the campus was Herbert Parrish, who penned an article in 1929 titled "Religion Goes to College" for *Century Magazine*.[9] Although he signed his article with only his first and last name, Herbert Parrish was the Reverend Dr. Herbert Parrish, an Episcopal minister who had recently retired from a twelve-year appointment as rector of the Episcopal church in New Brunswick, New Jersey, less than twenty miles from Princeton.[10] Published shortly after the opening of the Princeton University Chapel, Parrish's article used the new chapel as a way to talk about the need to return emotion to the worship services of American colleges and universities. Parrish, with stinging rhetoric, asserted that encouraging the right religious feeling was far more important than instilling the right religious dogma in college students.[11] While Parrish's Episcopalian identity put him in a position to desire sensual religious spaces and rich worship services more than someone from Princeton's Presbyterian tradition, he claimed that architecture and the accompanying ritual and atmosphere were essential components to foster religious feeling in the university setting in particular. Parrish's call for religious reform through emotional appeal was a twentieth-century reincarnation of the nineteenth-century British Cambridge Camden Society and Oxford Movement.[12]

Reverend Parrish was on the one hand optimistic that religion on campus in the 1920s was making a turn for the better, noting the construction of chapels like Princeton's as a sign that religion on campus was making a comeback. Parrish pointed to a number of markers to show that religion in higher education had declined since the late nineteenth century: the rise of nondenominational public universities created by the 1862 Morrill Act; the ending of compulsory chapel, beginning at Harvard in 1886; the publication in 1896 of Cornell University president Andrew Dickson White's *A History of the Warfare of Science with Theology in Christendom*, which pitted science against religion; and the attempts of the Carnegie Fund in 1905 to divorce colleges and universities from their denominational memberships in exchange for pension support. But "now suddenly religion is coming back again," he wrote, and none too soon, as "education without religion tended to put the sources of power into the hands of people who had no inhibitions, no morals, no prejudices." In a quip that conveyed the anxieties of many a university president and leader, Parrish warned, "A world of educated devils is not a pleasant thing to contemplate."[13]

While Parrish praised the steps being taken to return religion to higher education, he abhorred the kind of worship then prevalent on the college and university campus, saying it "suffered from the atrophied form of chapel worship that was both barren and dull to the limit." Echoing common complaints, he stated that compulsory chapel was so poor that it was "a small wonder that the boys come in looking like a bunch of convicts driven by their keepers, shuffling, reading books during the exercises, playing craps behind the seats with discretion, howling out the hymns as a relief to jaded nerves. The average chapel services are good for nobody."[14]

To save religion on the campus—to correct the damage done by spiritually poor worship services and uninspiring architecture—Parrish argued that universities needed to concentrate on the emotional rather than intellectual experience of religion. "In fact," Parrish wrote, "religion at college requires a very special treatment, if it is to survive, such as it has seldom had in America among Protestants." Parrish believed that religion in the academy needed to be regarded as "not merely a matter for study and reasoning" but also "a matter of emotion and conduct."[15] He privileged emotion over any kind of rational understanding of religion for the university student, whose vulnerability to attacks on religion and theology heightened the need for an emotional connection to religion.

To stir the emotions, universities needed the right kind of religious architecture. For Herbert Parrish as for a number of university leaders and architects, the powerful sensual cues of Gothic architecture held the greatest promise for reigniting religious fervor and competing with secular distractions, more than other iterations of historical architecture like Colonial Revival and Beaux Arts. Gothic buildings, and those modeled after them, trafficked in a sense of history, permanence, and romanticism about the height of Christianity's reach. Parrish characterized Gothic architecture, the centuries-long "exterior symbol of spiritual things," as having "an inevitable emotional effect." The power of Gothic architecture lay in its architecture, its atmosphere, and its associated ritual. Spatially, its scale dwarfed the worshipper. Its extreme verticality forced observation upward, heavenward. Atmospherically, Gothic architecture reveled in a sense of mystery and the senses—sight, smell, and sound. The emotional effect was the sum of these experiences. As Parrish described it, "The iteration of certain phrases, the atmosphere of a sacred place, the association with a devout group, the frequent contact with an impressive ritual, the imposed inspiration of sights, sounds and odors redolent of holy associations" associated with Gothic architecture could not "fail to produce emotions and to move to action in the direction of ideas and ideals indicated."[16]

The new Princeton University Chapel provided just that kind of atmosphere (fig. 2.1).[17] Following a 1920 fire that destroyed Princeton's Marquand Chapel, an eclectic Victorian confection designed by Richard Morris Hunt, architect Ralph Adams Cram with partner Frank Ferguson created a chapel whose architectural image was based "on that of the 14th century in England," though it was also influenced by the French Gothic.[18] Its exterior buttresses, finials, and sculpture asserted a definite Gothic vision to the campus. In the interior, the nave walls followed the Gothic arrangement of arcade, triforium, and clerestory (fig. 2.2). A proposed chancel screen separated the nave from

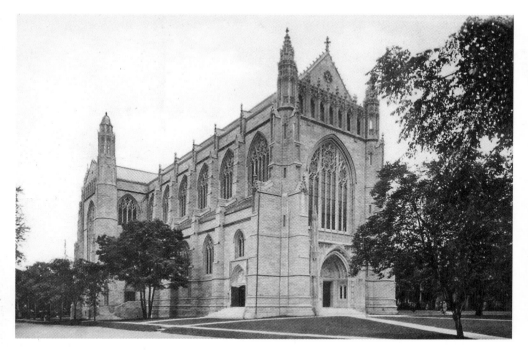

Figure 2.1. Princeton University Chapel, Cram & Ferguson, 1925–28, Princeton University. From box SP02, item 454, Princeton University Archives, Department of Rare Books and Special Collections, Princeton University Library.

the eastern third of the chapel, to be used as both a choir and as a daily chapel following the plan of Cambridge University's King's College Chapel, though the screen was not included in the final construction. As a concession to the importance of the spoken word to Protestant worship, one version of the chapel design positioned the pulpit at the very center on axis with the central aisle. However, the donation of an elaborate antique French pulpit caused the pulpit to be moved to the side, originally projecting into the first pew row. The altar at the back of the chancel became the terminal figure of the central aisle. Cram and Ferguson also asserted that the chapel "cannot be a bare and mechanistic auditorium," and they crafted an interior that included stained glass and ornament.[19] So effective was Cram and Ferguson's design that

Figure 2.2. Interior view of the Princeton University Chapel, 1932. From box MP30, item 771, Princeton University Archives, Department of Rare Books and Special Collections, Princeton University Library.

one could easily mistake their chapel for an authentic Gothic cathedral in Europe. It seemed of another age and another land.[20]

For Cram, the choice of the neo-Gothic style for the chapel served multiple ends. It provided the kind of atmosphere that Cram, a High Church Episcopalian, preferred, and it celebrated the golden age of Christianity. It reasserted the fundamental connection between education and religion or, in Cram's equivalent term, character. Cram was a leading practitioner and advocate of neo-Gothic architecture in

America, the leading member of the American Gothicists who, in the same vein as the nineteenth-century English critics Augustus Welby Northmore Pugin and John Ruskin, believed that a return to medieval architecture and art and craft could reform society.[21] He was also a disciple of Henry Vaughan, the British architect through whom the Victorian Gothic of the late nineteenth century would be transmuted to the more mature, archaeologically correct neo-Gothic of the twentieth century in the United States. Cram believed that collegiate architecture (as opposed to Gothic architecture in general) had reached its pinnacle in the fifteenth-, sixteenth-, and early-seventeenth-century architecture at England's universities and schools. Though adept in designing in many styles, Cram advocated the use of Gothic style for university architecture because "it is the only style that absolutely expresses our new-old, crescent ideals of an education that makes for culture and makes for character."[22] And for Cram, character included a strong religious and moral component—an essential, inseparable component of education vitally important to civilization—as he outlined in a 1912 address before the Royal Institute of British Architects:

> The foundations of sane and sound and wholesome society are neither industrial supremacy, nor world-wide trade, nor hoarded wealth; they are personal honor, clean living, fearlessness in action, self-reliance, generosity of impulse, good-fellowship, obedience to law, reverence and the fear of God—all those elements which are implied in the word "Character," which is the end of education and which is the proudest product of the old English residential college, and of the old English educational idea that brought it into being, maintained it for centuries, and holds it now a bulwark against the tides of anarchy and materialism that threaten the very endurance of civilisation itself.[23]

The neo-Gothic importantly aligned Princeton with the "old English educational ideal" of educating the whole person. As Princeton's campus architect, Cram had created a master plan in 1908 that imagined Princeton as the American Oxbridge. The chapel's neo-Gothic architecture was part of an ambitious neo-Gothic building program for residential quadrangles, libraries, and classroom buildings. In 1896, during the sesquicentennial celebration that marked the official name change from the College of New Jersey to Princeton University, the Princeton trustees decreed that all future Princeton buildings would be in the neo-Gothic style, emulating the medieval architecture of Oxford and Cambridge. Neo-Gothic architecture simultaneously symbolized Princeton's new preceptorial program modeled after the Oxbridge tutorial system in which students worked closely under professors to "transform thoughtless boys performing tasks into thinking men, fit for the work of the world"; appropriated the prestige of Oxbridge; and, in Princeton president Woodrow Wilson's oft-quoted line, "added a thousand years to the history of Princeton."[24] So close had the image of the Princeton campus come to that of an English university that in 1925 the *Princeton Alumni Weekly* published a photographic essay comparing the buildings of Princeton and Cambridge University, including a comparison of King's College Chapel and the proposed Princeton chapel.[25] Indeed, at institutions like Princeton, Yale, Duke, and the University of Pittsburgh under the steady hand of such architects as Cram, James Gamble Rogers, Horace Trumbauer, and Charles Klauder, the American campus in the interwar decades was shaped into an idealized version of Oxford and Cambridge.

But for the Princeton University Chapel itself, the choice of the neo-Gothic had implications beyond the imitation of Oxbridge for pedagogical reasons: it had significant practical and theological implications as well. For historically Protestant universities, the focus of Reverend Herbert Parrish's writing, the prescription of an essentially Catholic or Anglo-Catholic worship space for the university audience was, for some, a dissonant and uncomfortable proposition. Protestantism set itself apart from the Roman Catholic tradition in its emphasis on the spoken word over ritual and a preference for austere worship spaces over sanctuaries filled with figurative paintings, stained glass, and incense. Although by the 1920s Princeton had nearly as many Episcopal as Presbyterian students, the desire to remember Princeton's historic Presbyterian identity remained.

Charles Candee, a Princeton alumnus and minister, was among those who believed a chapel modeled on Catholic churches contradicted Princeton's religious tradition. While Candee sympathized with the desire to create an evocative religious interior, he strongly disagreed that the proposed chapel could meet the functional needs of a Protestant service. He wrote, "I know how very well how much real 'atmosphere' is created by the material surrounding of the sanctuary and how greatly such an atmosphere assists in the making of the spiritual impression the minister desires. But this beauty must be in keeping with the purposes of the service and must not run counter to them."[26] From Candee's perspective, the proposed chapel did nothing to accommodate the preaching aspect of the Protestant service. He vigorously disagreed with Cram and Ferguson's assertion that the longitudinal, Latin cross form of the proposed chapel "naturally . . . gives the best practical results, both in point of seeing and hearing[,] . . . since the great churches of the Middle Ages were conceived and constructed with particular reference to great preaching services,"[27] arguing instead that the form of Gothic churches promoted ritual, not preaching.

Another alumnus wrote of the dissonant presence of an altar in the chapel plans and wondered what one was to do with it:

> There is a place in this plan where there ought to be an altar. If we put nothing there, won't the whole thing look bobtailed? If we put a sodafountain there, it will look ridiculous. If we put an altar there, our preachers will have to regard it. Either they will make believe they don't see it, which will shock the Episcopal contingent, or they will pretend they are quite used to it, which will make them ridiculous. That is the difficulty with this plan; it will force us to shout aloud either for or against the Catholic Church.[28]

Simply, the chapel that Cram and Ferguson proposed was strikingly out of sync with Protestant worship. As Candee wrote, "Our conceptions of religion and of worship are not exactly those of the 14th century. Princeton has been and is Protestant." Given the failure of the Gothic form to accommodate Protestant worship, he wondered, "what right have we to build a chapel which is utterly unfit for the Reformed mode of service?"[29]

One senior Princetonian, John A. Clinton Gray, put the distinction between Protestant and Catholic worship in terms of a stark opposition between the rational and the emotional. Gray asserted that the hallmark of Protestantism was its intellectual, rational appeal, while the hallmark of Catholicism was its revelry in mystery, emotion, and irrationality. To use a Gothic, Catholic environment for Protestant worship, Gray argued, confused the nature of Protestantism altogether: "Now if there is one thing for which a Gothic cathedral stands — and our Chapel is to be virtually a Gothic Cathedral — it is the mystery of religion, and if there is one thing for which Presbyterian Princeton stands it is Protestantism." The Catholic-associated Gothic style "stands for an appeal to the senses, and not to the intellect, which is Protestantism's chief claim to fame."[30] "For in a Gothic building," Gray continued, "the individual who seeks to express himself rationally is guilty of bad taste."[31] The Princeton trustees of "bygone days" would turn in "their graves at the thought of the substitution of Popish splendor for the purposely unappealing conventicler [religious meeting] of Colonial America." Gray imagined the trustees asking, "How will the student be able to fasten his intellectual attention upon the sermon, or upon the common-sense prayer when the whole atmosphere of the place pleads for a forgetfulness of self in a state of absorption in the divine?"[32]

This choice of the emotional over the intellectual engagement with religion was at the heart of Parrish's proposal. Anticipating resistance to his assertion of the primacy of emotion in religious worship as "mere self-hypnotism, an unintellectual substitute for right thinking," Parrish asked a central question about recasting religion on campus in emotional terms: "Why may not self-hypnotism, the deliberate stirring of the emotions, be quite as divine, as valid a method of influencing character and conduct as analytical thought . . . ?"[33] Parrish wrote that religion gave "hope, courage, peace, joy and contentment to multitudes," emotional qualities that were "powerful" and "invaluable" and should not be allowed to "evaporate into the thin air of critical intellectuality in our colleges."[34] For Parrish as for other Protestants, the emotional appeal to religion was precisely the route to reengage students in worship in an era of cultural secularization: "Hours of talking cannot do what a glimpse will accomplish. Hence thoughtful people are realizing that the modern world needs something beside motion-pictures, needs cathedrals and Gothic chapels, to impress the imagination of susceptible youth and the masses."[35]

Aligning religion with emotion also set religion apart from science. In the context of the university, religion could claim authority over what science could not: feeling. This idea that religion depended on the emotions rather than the intellect was a sea change in the early twentieth century. The historian Julie Reuben argues that by the 1920s American academics had accepted "that science excluded values and that morality was determined by feeling rather than intellect."[36] Rather than challenge science's authority over the intellect, Parrish wished to capitalize on religion's potential to reach students through feeling. Claiming the emotional life was one avenue for religion to reclaim some authority and even usefulness.

Herbert Parrish was not alone in this assessment that religion on campus was best served by appealing to the emotions. At the laying of the cornerstone at the University of Chicago's neo-Gothic chapel in 1926, the philosopher and professor James Hayden Tufts reconciled the place of emotion and religion with the dominant intellectual climate in the university. Though "religion in a university chapel may not forget the scientific spirit and mistake emotion for intelligent and resolute endeavor," Tufts reasoned, the appeal to the emotions through art had its proper place. Weary students needed "nothing so much as the deeper and ordered rhythms of noble music, the poet's imagery, the conflicts and stresses resolved, and all the influences transmitted through the arts which in such a building will find a fitting home." The feelings and senses that students absorbed through the experience of worship in a neo-Gothic church, accompanied by music and ritual, would "open a way to the experience of God."[37]

The Princeton University Chapel did have this effect, at least for some students. On the chapel's opening, one Princetonian explained that the chapel was so beautiful, so spiritually satisfying, that the compulsion to worship was no longer necessary, confirming Reverend

Parrish's contention that the emotional appeal was more effective than the intellectual:

> Given the new Chapel, he [the average Princeton undergraduate] is wondering whether the coercive measure will be rescinded, and whether the Chapel services will not be made so beautiful, in proportion to the new surroundings, that his own aesthetic sense will urge him to attend. For, after all, it must be admitted that the sensuous impressions to be gotten from the Chapel and all that surrounds it will be more influential in elevating the spiritual being of the average undergraduate than any doctrines which may be expounded therin.[38]

Parrish saw the new Princeton University Chapel as a step in the right direction, but the worship services did not go far enough in exhausting the emotional possibilities. Parrish believed the chapel needed the addition of more color, lamps, shrines, religious images, and rich, ritualistic services but realized that "you cannot expect all this yet at a university where the Presbyterian traditions prevail."[39] Cram too called for reform of university worship services, claiming that "youth has a sufficient sense of saving humor to realize and resent the miscegenation of a chapel as beautiful as those of Oxford and Cambridge and a liturgy as empty and soporific as one finds in some moribund conventicler of the more Puritan persuasion."[40]

What these university chapels rendered in a lavish Gothic image and in large scale did accomplish on their own was to reassert a stalwart physical presence of religion, one seductive to the senses and the emotions, even as religion on campus was being challenged.

LOCATING RELIGION ON CAMPUS

The buildings located at the campus center presented a moment to define, clarify, and proclaim the values the modern American university held supreme. In 1930, the values that the Yale campus conveyed made some people nervous. An enormous new library at the new campus center was under construction, and the university had also recently devoted large sums to a cathedral-like gymnasium. However, there was no new chapel. What did this communicate about the university's values? As Yale president James Rowland Angell summarized, a new chapel at the campus center would be "a natural completion to a scale of values" that those in favor of religion at Yale felt was "somewhat distorted."[1] The center, especially important in the context of Beaux Arts planning methods, was crucial to defining a university's values.

This chapter examines the development of the campus core at Johns Hopkins University, Harvard University, and Yale University to illustrate that campus planning was another critical tool in the attempt to craft a sustained presence of religion in the university. These campus plans also show the architectural and spatial connections often made between the chapel and the library at the center to communicate the university's desired scale of values. While science was a growing power in the university's intellectual life, it was not represented directly in the campus center. Rather, the library stood as a proxy for empirical knowledge at the center, and for many it needed to be balanced by the chapel as a symbol of revealed knowledge to make visible the university's core beliefs. But these campus plans were realized with varying degrees of success. Harvard managed to architecturally balance the chapel and the library on Harvard Yard, yet this was contrary to the belief of many of its alumni that Harvard was in fact an institution divorced from religion. While Johns Hopkins and Yale imagined chapels at the center of their campuses, their failure to see such spaces constructed, whether for financial reasons or an implicit apathy toward religion, made visible the changing and declining influence of religion in the modern American university.

JOHNS HOPKINS UNIVERSITY

That there is no chapel at the center of Johns Hopkins University seems expected and even natural. Johns Hopkins, founded in 1876, claims the accolade as the first university in the United States to follow the German model of higher education—focused on rigorous intellectual and scientific inquiry and graduate education—that was the goal of reform movements of the American college in the late nineteenth century. Its association with the German research model implied that religious ideals were far from Johns Hopkins's concerns, and mid-twentieth-century historiography of American higher education took up this supposition. In his history on American higher education, published in 1962, Frederick Rudolph cast Johns Hopkins as prototypical of what happens to religion once research becomes supreme: "For the acceptance of revealed religious truth the new university in Baltimore substituted a search for scientific truth. For preparation for life in the next world it substituted a search for an understanding of this world."[2] Johns Hopkins's Homewood campus in Baltimore appears to confirm this interpretation. The monumental neo-Colonial library and academic building at the campus center and the absence of a university chapel suggest that religion did not figure among Johns Hopkins University's priorities.

Such assumptions are wrong. The university charter required that Johns Hopkins be nonsectarian in keeping with the beliefs of the Quakers, who had counted benefactor Johns Hopkins among its members and who comprised a large portion of the university's board of trustees. But this did not exclude the practice of religion. Founding president Daniel Coit Gilman himself led the voluntary morning worship service at the school's original downtown campus, promoted the activities of the Young Men's Christian Association, and became president of the American Bible Society.[3] Although some historians point to the opening ceremony of Johns Hopkins University in 1876 at which the noted agnostic and Darwin advocate Thomas Henry Huxley spoke and at which no prayer was given as evidence of Hopkins's eschewal of religion,[4] in fact a prayer was offered at the inauguration of President Gilman in 1876, and the bishop of Baltimore gave a benediction at the opening of the new Homewood campus in 1915.[5] Recent revisions to the history of Johns Hopkins in the canon of American higher education reveal that the university was not inimical to religion, as is often supposed.[6] Hopkins's focus on science was not in itself a rejection of religion. Gilman even stated that Johns Hopkins University had always "been conducted as a Christian institution, not as ecclesiastical or sectarian on the one hand, nor as without religious character on the other hand."[7]

Religion was originally to have a prominent architectural expression in the new Johns Hopkins University campus. Though formal worship space did not exist in its original downtown Baltimore campus (a patchwork of buildings the university acquired over time), a chapel was intended for the university's new campus in northern Baltimore. In 1902, benefactors William Wyman and William Keyser gave the university the Homewood estate, which included the Federal-style Carroll mansion once owned by a signer of the Declaration of Independence, Charles Carroll. In 1904, Johns Hopkins president Ira Remsen, Gilman's successor, and the trustees held an architectural competition for the Homewood campus master plan. Of the five firms invited to create the vision of the new Johns Hopkins, the Baltimore architects J. Harleston Parker and Douglas H. Thomas, in conjunction with the landscape architect Warren Manning, were chosen as the firm that had best positioned the buildings outlined in the competition guidelines.[8] Those guidelines included a provision for a chapel with a "monumental character"—at least six thousand square feet and accommodating at least five hundred worshippers.[9]

The classic Beaux Arts arrangement of Parker and Thomas's plan for Homewood reserved a place of special importance for the chapel. Their scheme organized the new Hopkins buildings on major and minor axes (fig. 3.1). The principal academic and laboratory buildings linked by a colonnade lined the plan's major axis, running roughly north-south and parallel to fashionable Charles Street. An enormous library stood at the northern end, and a large museum anchored the opposite end. This axis was internal, visible only when the student or visitor stepped inside the campus boundaries. The shorter, minor axis presented the institution's public face to the entrance orthogonal to Charles Street. As students and visitors came from Charles Street, up the circle drive known as the "bowl," and past the Carroll mansion, they were to enter through ceremonial gates to the sight of an enormous domed chapel across an open quadrangle—a vision evocatively rendered by the firm in a drawing showing the dome of the chapel rising as a shadow behind the entrance gates (fig. 3.2).

Parker and Thomas's design for the chapel was an appropriate answer to the requirement that the chapel have a monumental character. A pedimented narthex fronted the rectangular sanctuary terminating in an apse. A cupola surmounted the tall dome ringed with columns, echoing the grandeur of the U.S. Capitol. This dome gave the chapel greater prominence in the skyline over the library's low, Pantheon-like dome. Two museums to either side of the chapel formed the chapel forecourt. The plan emphasized religion's importance to the university even to those who only passed by on Charles Street. It also uniquely balanced the importance of religion and learning to students and faculty, who would see the chapel on entry to the university but would focus on the library while coming and going from the laboratories. Far from ignoring religion, the plans for the new Johns Hopkins celebrated it.

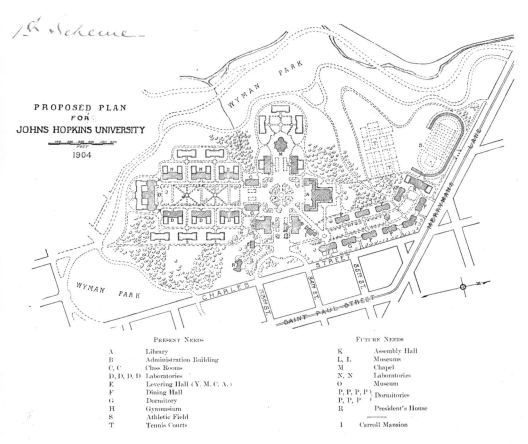

Figure 3.1. First scheme of the Johns Hopkins University campus master plan by Parker & Thomas with Warren Manning, 1904. From box 1, "Homewood Campus Printed Material," MS 137, Special Collections, Sheridan Libraries, Johns Hopkins University.

Action on Parker and Thomas's campus plan languished between 1905 and 1912 due to lack of funds. The financial situation forced a reconsideration of the university's priorities in building the new campus in 1912. Academic and residential buildings received top priority; the architects Grosvenor Atterbury and Frank Miles Day, who served on the campus plan advisory board, classified these buildings as "immediately

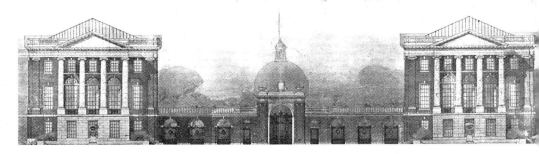

Figure 3.2. Drawing of proposed entrance to Johns Hopkins University show-ing the dome of the chapel in the background. From box 1, "Homewood Cam-pus Printed Material," MS 137, Special Collections, Sheridan Libraries, Johns Hopkins University.

essential." These essential buildings included, in descending order of importance, the power plant; the main academic building and library; laboratories for chemistry, geology, physics, and biology; and a stu-dent hall, dormitory, dining hall, and gymnasium. In a second group of buildings described as "desirable for the near future," the chapel ranked second behind buildings for the undergraduates but trumped such buildings as a president's house, a faculty club, an astronomical observatory, an administration building and assembly hall, a museum, and engineering buildings.[10]

The reordering of priorities for Johns Hopkins's campus plan, if for practical and financial reasons, displaced the chapel from the cam-pus center. Rather than erecting a chapel to encapsulate the ideal of the university, the revised 1912 plan from Parker and Thomas, now with partner Arthur Wallace Rice, instead positioned Gilman Hall at the entrance axis to the university. The geology, biology, chemistry, and physics laboratories further defined the central quadrangle visible from Charles Street. Gilman Hall, named for the university's first president, combined academic spaces for the humanities, including history, phi-losophy, and languages, along with the principal library of the university. The building also assumed the memorial functions typically assigned to the chapel, including a room dedicated to the memory of Daniel

Coit Gilman. The building presented a monumental facade for the entrance to Johns Hopkins. Cast in the image of Independence Hall, complete with a 120-foot clock tower and classical portico, and with references to the Carroll mansion, Gilman Hall—the largest building on campus—was, as Johns Hopkins University librarian M. Llewellyn Raney described, "the capitol of the campus."[11]

Although the new Johns Hopkins University campus would not have a chapel, the university did erect a building for the Young Men's Christian Association, Levering Hall. But even here the expression of religion was compromised. Whereas in the earlier plans of 1904 and 1906 Levering Hall was placed prominently in the bowl entrance to the university near the Carroll mansion, ultimately the structure was placed below and behind the central quadrangle. Architecturally, the Johns Hopkins University campus did not express the original desire to make religion a prominent part of its campus or visually affirm President Daniel Coit Gilman's claim that Johns Hopkins was a Christian university.

The lack of a chapel building reflected a more complicated revolution underfoot at Johns Hopkins. As George Marsden argues, though Gilman publicly proclaimed the importance of religion or a generalized morality especially with regard to undergraduate education and character building, the real experiment of graduate and professional education at Johns Hopkins University divorced religion from the search for empirical truth. In a process Marsden calls "methodological secularization," the isolation of certain questions or problems promoted mechanisms for solving them that had little to do with religious concerns. Therefore, "when entering the laboratory, pious Christians were expected to leave their religious beliefs at the door, even if they had prayed God to bless their work and came from their discoveries praising God for his work."[12] Such a division had powerful consequences even outside of the laboratory. "Since the laboratory became a key metaphor and model for all advanced intellectual work," Marsden contends, "this ideal was extended throughout the university."[13]

However, Gilman and others did not believe value-free science presented an attack on Christianity since scientific investigation often was undertaken in service to the greater good. Religion and science were simply two different means to the same end. As Gilman said at his inauguration, "Religion claims to interpret the word of God, and science to reveal the laws of God," echoing the liberal Protestant belief that all discovery of truth revealed God and allied the work of the laboratory with worship within a chapel.[14] While Johns Hopkins University's early leaders may have been confident in this belief in religion's endemic role to the work of the university, the fact that the campus does not have a chapel at its center conveys something else about the university's values. Despite what was intended, the library and laboratories instead of a chapel at the university center remain the enduring image of Johns Hopkins, leading many, like the historian Frederick Rudolph, to surmise that Johns Hopkins University valued religion not at all.

HARVARD UNIVERSITY

Where the absence of a chapel at Johns Hopkins belies the university's early attitudes toward religion, the presence of a large new church on Harvard Yard made plain the Harvard administration's desire to see religion at the center of campus despite vocal alumni opposition. For Harvard University president Abbott Lawrence Lowell, the new church was vitally important in properly balancing religion in the university. As we have already seen, the size of the new church was an advertisement of religion's continuing importance to Harvard's educational mission. From a planning perspective, the construction of a large new church also served to create symbolic balance with the hulking new library at Harvard's center. By constructing a church that could architecturally answer the grandeur and authority of the library, the Harvard administration in the interwar decades ensured that the heart of campus conveyed Harvard's values — at least as conceived by its leadership — to the Harvard community.

The construction of a new church at Harvard University as a memorial to Harvard's World War I dead provided a flashpoint for controversy in the 1920s. For some Harvard alumni, who were funding the war memorial, the idea that religion still held a place of importance at

Harvard was jarring. Harvard was the first institution to end its compulsory chapel services in 1886, a move that confirmed, they believed, that Harvard was a lay institution divorced from religion.

For President Lowell and supporters of the church, Harvard was not in fact divorced from religion. And no other proposed forms for the memorial—including a memorial shaft, a memorial auditorium, a carillon tower, a dormitory quadrangle, and a gymnasium—could express the sacrifice made by these Harvard men as strongly as a church. Lowell, a Unitarian, believed in the direct correlation between religion and serving one's country and the broader good, and a memorial church was the only appropriate articulation of this relationship in his view. As he stated in a letter published in the *Harvard Alumni Bulletin* and such newspapers as the *Boston Evening Transcript*, "If the need of the American colleges, and the object of a war memorial, is to develop a stronger and more positive moral consciousness of the duty of public service, then it cannot be divorced from religion; and religion, as all the ages have shown, is, like everything else, assisted by an appropriate physical expression." The memorial church would embody "our aspiration towards moral character."[15]

President Lowell's support for the church was also in keeping with his belief that the university had a responsibility to instruct its students in the higher aspects of life. As World War I ended, Lowell argued that "among the strongest agencies" to prevent the "materialistic reaction" that often accompanied the end of wars "ought to be our colleges and universities, which should feel more than ever their duty to keep before the minds of young men the eternal values and the spiritual truths that endure when material things pass away."[16] The university and the war memorial were the proper settings to remind students of these values and truths.

Yet as is evident in letters of strident protest in the *Harvard Alumni Bulletin*, some alumni believed a religious memorial was problematic from a number of perspectives. First was religion's relationship both to the war and to the teaching of morality. Several alumni balked at the assertion that religion had anything to do with the war or the patriotism that inspired the war dead to fight for the cause.[17] When Lowell asserted that the church was to teach morality to the Harvard students, some alumni responded that it was the classroom, not the church, from which the principles of religion and morality more broadly should be taught. Second was the issue of religious sensitivity and equality. Among the World War I dead the memorial was to honor were Jews and, presumably, atheists, making the proposed Christian and generically Protestant church incongruent with and insulting to their beliefs. One alumnus, an admitted non-Christian, wondered why the memorial had to stand for Christian principles among all others and challenged President Abbot Lawrence Lowell's very premise for the church that morality and religion were necessarily intertwined.[18] Some alumni plainly refuted the arguments that Harvard needed a new church to provide more worship space.[19] Simply, the opponents of the church saw no need for a new religious space on the campus. They argued against the very idea that a war memorial needed to have a religious meaning and that Harvard in particular and university training in general needed to have a religious connection.[20]

Such vocal opposition to the church and to religion, however, came too late. The memorial church, first proposed by the Associated Harvard Clubs in 1924, captured the endorsement of the Harvard Alumni Association, the Harvard Board of Overseers, and the Corporation of Harvard College. By 1928, some 25,000 donors had given over $750,000 for the memorial.[21] After nearly a decade of argument among alumni and university leaders, the Harvard Memorial Church, to be completed in 1931, was chosen as Harvard's war memorial.

Lowell and others seized on the construction of the war memorial to implement a comprehensive plan for Harvard, which unlike most American universities in the early twentieth century had yet to execute a reordering of its campus. Lowell agreed with former Harvard overseer W. Cameron Forbes's colorful mandate that "we ought to have no more higgly piggly building at Cambridge," and he believed that, before the war memorial could be positioned, a "complete scheme . . . ought to be made, and adhered to hereafter as closely as possible."[22] Other long-term plans for Harvard had been attempted but never carried out. In 1896, under the presidency of Charles Eliot, a subcommittee of the Board of Overseers commissioned Olmsted, Olmsted & Eliot to design a master plan for Harvard. The firm provided a plan replete with Beaux Arts vistas from Harvard Yard south to the Charles River.[23] The architectural critic Montgomery Schuyler suggested in 1909 that Harvard simply pick up and move its buildings like pawns on a chessboard to create the appropriate axial vistas.[24]

But in spite of the popularity of Beaux Arts planning in university master plans of this era, Lowell believed these principles were not suited to Harvard. The "conventional boulevard and main axis" of the Beaux Arts plan, he said, would be "impossible here [at Harvard] without destroying practically everything that connects us with the past." Lowell believed "the principle of the cloister rather than the public park; the secluded precinct rather than the open approach" should be the guiding rule for Harvard's master plan.[25] In 1922, the university asked Charles Coolidge, whose firm Coolidge, Shepley, Bulfinch and Abbot became Harvard's house architects under Lowell and would design the new Harvard Memorial Church, to create a campus master plan along these cloistral lines.[26]

If Beaux Arts was not to order Harvard's campus as a whole, it played an important part in defining the center of Harvard, where the library and the church—knowledge and religion—were to be positioned in rigidly axial and equal terms. The construction of Widener Library (1913–15) introduced an immense Beaux Arts building to Harvard Yard. A memorial to Harry Elkins Widener, a Harvard student who was lost on the *Titanic*, and designed by the Philadelphia architect Horace Trumbauer as specified by the donor, Widener's mother, the massive library presented an imposing classical facade to Harvard Yard (fig. 3.3). Its monumental flight of stairs led to a screen of twelve Corinthian columns protecting the enormous store of knowledge beyond. The new library announced Harvard's identity as a modern university, where the attainment of knowledge appeared limitless. The library was a temple of knowledge.

Widener Library made its counterpart across the Yard, Appleton Chapel, seem paltry by comparison (fig. 3.4). Erected in 1856 as the second freestanding chapel in Harvard's history, Appleton Chapel occupied the northern end of Harvard Yard. The chapel's main western entrance, marked with an off-center tower, was originally oriented to the Old Yard and specifically to the old Holden Chapel.[27] The chapel's

Figure 3.3. Widener Library, Horace Trumbauer, 1913, Harvard University. Courtesy of Harvard University Archives, HUV 49 (19–4a).

long nave elevation made little nod to the rear of Widener Library's predecessor, the Gothic revival Gore Hall, to the south. But within thirteen years of the chapel's construction, its siting was significantly compromised. The construction of the Thayer Hall dormitory in 1869 in front of Appleton Chapel placed the chapel's main entrance uncomfortably close to the back of the dormitory.[28] From the open space of Harvard Yard, the principal view of the chapel was not of its entrance but of the side of its nave.

The construction of Widener Library only exacerbated the poor siting of the chapel. Whereas the previous Gore Hall had ignored the Yard, facing outward to Massachusetts Avenue, Widener Library now

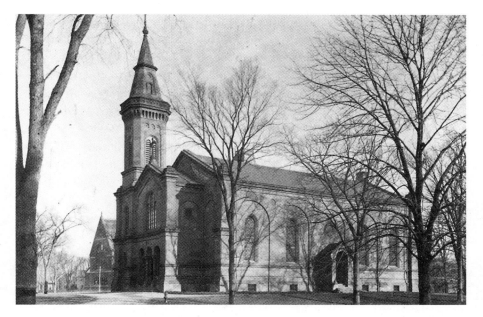

Figure 3.4. View of the southern elevation of Appleton Chapel (1853) facing Widener Library. Courtesy of Harvard University Archives, HUV 53 (1–1a).

turned inward toward the Yard. Widener demanded a commensurate architectural response from Appleton, one it could not give. Already maligned for its outdated aesthetics, Appleton had only a small shed over a single side door to its nave to answer Widener's massive, raised, twelve-column portico entrance (see fig. 3.4). In scale, the chapel shrank in the shadow of the library.

While the chapel supporters' arguments for the new memorial church chiefly centered on the fitting nature of a church for a war memorial, the architectural inequality between the library and the church — and the intimation that religion was second place — played an important role. Proof of the desire to create an appropriate expression of religion at Harvard was President Lowell's determination to place the new Harvard Memorial Church directly on the site of Appleton Chapel.[29] Lowell dismissed a proposal to position the chapel on the site of Quincy and Harvard Streets, which would have left the Widener-Appleton quandary unsolved and positioned religion still farther from the center of Harvard, deeming it too noisy. He firmly stated, "I do not believe there is any other good site, except that where Appleton Chapel now stands."[30] For Lowell, the construction of a new, more monumental church at the center of Harvard, opposite the new library, was critical. A committee appointed by the Board of Overseers also championed the Appleton Chapel site, saying it "expresses admirably the ideal fundamental to the University, with the chapel and the library facing each other."[31] University leaders wished to create the proper architectural balance of intellectual and spiritual life at Harvard in the twentieth century.

The firm Coolidge, Shepley, Bulfinch and Abbott did not fail in their effort to create a church very much an equal to Widener Library. In the literature promoting the church, its design was advertised in terms that guaranteed it would meet Widener's architecture and even surpass it. A pamphlet proposing the church as Harvard's war memorial assured that "its spire will dominate the quadrangle of lawn and elms reaching southward to Widener library" and that its "massive columns will so strengthen the form of the church that it will not be diminished by the size of the library across the lawn."[32] What the architects could not achieve, however, was a different orientation from that of Appleton Chapel. By the 1930s, the site was hemmed in by Thayer Hall to the west, Robinson Hall to the east, and the original Fogg Museum to the north.[33] In order to preserve the open space characteristic of this side of Harvard Yard, the architects were forced to place the new church in nearly the same footprint as Appleton Chapel, with its entrance facade facing Thayer Hall and its nave elevation fronting Widener Library (fig. 3.5).

It was with the architects' handling of the nave elevation that Harvard Memorial Church succeeded where Appleton Chapel had failed (fig. 3.6). The memorial function of the church provided the opportunity to more appropriately align the chapel with the library. The architects positioned the memorial room, dedicated to the war dead, orthogonal to the nave along its side to create a monumental entrance to the church that also answered the entrance to Widener Library. The memorial room became the building's defining feature. Slightly set off

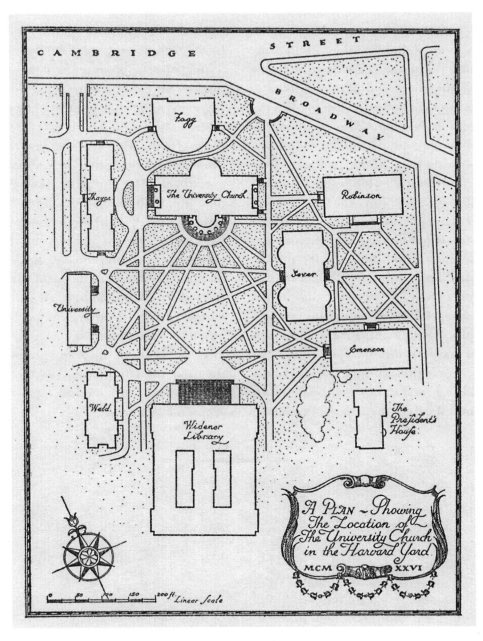

Figure 3.5. Plan of Harvard Yard showing location of proposed Harvard Memorial Church with projecting memorial room, 1926. Courtesy of Harvard University Archives, HUB 1555.2, box 1.

Figure 3.6. Harvard Memorial Church, Coolidge, Shepley, Bulfinch & Abbott, 1931. Courtesy of Harvard University Archives, HUV 53A (6–7a).

in a projection from the nave wall, a pedimented, tetrastyle Doric portico announced the memorial room to the Yard. The memorial room and portico gave dimension to the nave elevation, provided a central focal point, and asserted the church into the space of the Yard. The stair to the memorial room's entrance elevated the church above the Yard and signaled its importance. The relationship between the church and the library is further visually exaggerated. The portico and door to the memorial room, which was to be the students' entrance and from which the nave can also be reached, directly align with the portico and door of the library. The sidewalk that runs from one door to another also exaggerates the visual connection between the two buildings. The 170-foot spire that rises above the church adds a vertical thrust to the otherwise low-lying building, leaving no doubt to the prominence of religion in the Harvard skyline, and gives a sense of massiveness that equals the hulking footprint of the library. That the monumentality of the church sought to balance the monumentality of the library is clearly discernible.

The church and the library together define the space of Harvard Yard. As the architectural historian Banbridge Bunting described it, the church and the library form the "*skene* and *cavea* of a great unroofed theater."[34] The architects successfully created a monumental church on a scale large enough to answer Widener Library. At the center of Harvard, within its largest open space, and at the site of its commencements, knowledge and spirituality share an apparent equal footing. But this was accomplished by the will of President Lowell. Just how well the conception of the center of Harvard reflected the values and will of its students and alumni, even in the 1930s, is unclear. Harvard Memorial Church was an aggressive assertion of the vitality of religion at Harvard, and yet it can also be conceived as a desiccated symbol, a white elephant.

YALE UNIVERSITY

For Yale University, locating a chapel at the center of campus to emphasize the university's proper "scale of values" was long hoped for but never achieved.[35] The ambitious replanning of Yale in the early twentieth century offered an opportunity to place religion at the very heart of campus, and architects conceived of a center with a chapel and the library balancing each other, just as at Harvard. The inability to locate a traditional religious form at the center of Yale placed a new layer of meaning on the neo-Gothic library, which became both library and chapel, and confirmed religion's shifting role on Yale's campus.

Religion figured prominently in Yale's early history. Yale's earliest buildings, forming a line called Old Brick Row, faced three churches on the New Haven Green, and the college itself had two freestanding chapels. In the second half of the nineteenth century, Yale began to move away from this linear conception of campus planning. In an effort to wall itself off from the city of New Haven and create an inward-focused campus, Yale implemented a building scheme to create a large quadrangle bounded by College, Chapel, Elm, and High Streets. The buildings placed at the edges of the block were to define the quadrangle, with a large green space reserved for the middle. Part of Yale's expansion to this quadrangle was the construction of the new Battell Chapel.[36]

Timothy Dwight, a professor of divinity who would assume the presidency of Yale in 1886, saw a tremendous opportunity for the physical expression of religion at Yale with the construction of Battell Chapel in the 1870s. Dwight argued that the very middle of the quadrangle was the most appropriate location for the chapel. He believed that the chapel should be "as central as possible" so that "it may by its very position, remind every observer that all things in the education here are designed to lead the soul to that which is higher and better."[37] This proposal was intriguing: To place a chapel at the center, surround it with green space, and ring it with a wall of buildings would leave no doubt as to the prominence given to religion. As Dwight stated, "The placing of the house of religious worship for the university at the central point of all the other edifices will be one means of defending and preserving the true faith here. . . . [T]he turning and pointing of all things will be *visibly* toward religion."[38] But this vision went unrealized. The Victorian Gothic Battell Chapel (1874–76), designed by Russell Sturgis Jr., was instead shoved into the northeast corner of the quadrangle, subsumed into the line of the residential buildings. The apse was the chapel's most prominent feature, and only this was visible on the outer, public side of the quadrangle.[39] Rather than highlighted as an essential building in Yale's program, Battell Chapel was, from a planning point of view, muted.

The replanning of Yale provided a new opportunity to prominently position religion among the university buildings. In 1919, a Yale alumnus, Francis Garvan, commissioned the architect John Russell Pope to create a master plan, which Pope published as *Yale University: A Plan for Its Future Buildings*, an extravagantly illustrated, large folio with drawings by Otto Eggers.[40] This master plan had enormous importance for Yale. Though Yale had announced its shift to university status in 1886, the idea of the university would come to maturity in the early twentieth century through its campus architecture.[41] The campus plan inaugurated an ambitious building program for Yale.

Pope, who had been trained at the École des Beaux Arts in Paris, created a plan that was the personification of Beaux Arts design. He proposed connecting the two parallel, rudimentary north-south axes in the Yale campus—one from the Campus (now Old Campus) to the Commons and the other from Sheffield Scientific School along Hillhouse Avenue—with a new east-west axis along Wall Street (fig. 3.7). This east-west axis, called New Campus and later renamed Cross Campus, was to become the new center of Yale. Pope proposed placing the largest of Yale's new buildings here at the most visible points. A new cathedral-like library with a massive tower was to be at the middle of New Campus, at the "centre of gravity, architectural and mentally, so to speak, of the University," and on axis with Old Campus.[42] With the proposed demolition of Durfee Hall, a great vista would connect these two parts of Yale, with the library as the focal point. The library, conceived along the lines of Cambridge University's King's College Chapel, fused the library and chapel in one building (fig. 3.8). While a new traditional worship space was not part of Pope's reinvention of Yale, his proposal of a library in the image of a Gothic cathedral both anticipated and informed the library-cathedral that James Gamble Rogers would ultimately design for the campus center.

The Yale Corporation appointed three architects as an advisory committee to evaluate Pope's proposal for the remaking of the Yale

Figure 3.7. Proposed master plan for Yale University, John Russell Pope, 1919, with Cross Campus at center left. From John Russell Pope, *Yale University: A Plan for Its Future Buildings* (New York: Cheltenham, 1919), RU 703, Manuscripts and Archives, Yale University Library.

campus. In February 1920, Paul Philippe Cret, also an École des Beaux-Arts–trained architect; Bertram Grosvenor Goodhue, former partner of Ralph Adams Cram and future architect of Yale's new library; and William Adams Delano, a Yale alumnus who had also designed several Yale buildings, submitted their critique of the plan. Their evaluation reconsidered the new center of Yale. Whereas Pope envisioned a large Beaux Arts axis along Wall Street that connected the new campus to the Hillhouse Avenue corridor, the advisory committee recommended shortening the axis to extend only from High to College Streets. This shortened axis, though still providing a large central space, transformed the new center of Yale from a grand boulevard to an enclosed quadrangle, dramatically altering Pope's intended effect.[43]

The advisory committee also reordered the buildings at the new center. Their recommendation was to put the library at the position of the gymnasium in the Pope plan and move the gymnasium to a secondary position to the south of the library. The library, then, would be located at a terminal end of the east-west axis of Cross Campus. More important, the architects advised that a new chapel be placed immediately

The Library

Figure 3.8. Drawing by Otto Eggers of John Russell Pope's proposed new Yale University library on Cross Campus. From *The Architecture of John Russell Pope*, vol. 1 (New York: Helburn, 1925), 39.

opposite the library. The juxtaposition of the chapel and the library in conversation with one another was an important communication of the values of Yale. As the Yale Corporation Architectural Plan Committee stated simply, "The buildings which represent most clearly and strongly the educational ideals of Yale are the new Chapel and the Library. For that reason, they should be placed in very prominent positions on the new Campus."[44] Also to be included at the center were the administration building, the dining hall, and Woolsey Hall, the large auditorium building. Since these buildings "should express to the graduates and under-graduates and the outside world the idea of the unity of the institution," they were to be "centrally located and near to each other."[45] In conceiving Yale's new center, the architects and planners gathered together the communal buildings of the university and also highlighted the two buildings that embodied the university identity: the chapel and the library.

The redesign and implementation of Yale's master plan fell to Rogers, who was appointed consulting architect to the university's general plan in November 1920.[46] From about 1920 to 1923, Rogers worked with civic leaders and Pope himself to produce a series of general university schemes in anticipation of nearly $20 million in building projects.[47] Following the advisory committee's advice, Rogers toned down the strong axial vistas of the Pope plan, retaining some views while closing off others. What Rogers's plan lost in visually uniting the far reaches of the university it gained in creating a well-defined campus center that embodied the priorities of Yale.[48]

Though Rogers produced several schemes for Cross Campus, the one most closely akin to its realization best articulates his complete idea for it (fig. 3.9).[49] At the westernmost end of the Cross Campus axis along High Street was the new Sterling Memorial Library. The large collegiate Gothic building, a memorial to Yale alumnus and benefactor John Sterling, was initially designed by Bertram Grosvenor Goodhue and then taken up by Rogers after Goodhue's death in 1924. The library stood at the head of a rectangular green space lined with symmetrically positioned dormitories and classrooms. A secondary and minor north-south axis cut through the middle of this green space, providing a visual and physical link with Woolsey Hall and the dining hall.

Figure 3.9. Perspective view of the proposed chapel (bottom) and library (top) for Yale's Cross Campus by James Gamble Rogers, 1924. From "The Plan for the Physical Development of Yale University," *Yale Alumni Weekly* (1 February 1924): 524, Manuscripts and Archives, Yale University Library.

Across from the library on Cross Campus was to be the chapel (see fig. 3.9). The chapel's proposed dimensions were dizzying. Its footprint included a nave 351 feet long and 90 feet wide, far exceeding the size of the new Princeton University Chapel realized at 277 feet long and 76 feet wide. The chapel was to accommodate up to five thousand worshippers, significantly larger than the roughly two-thousand-seat capacity of similar chapel projects at Princeton and the University of

Chicago. The chapel was to have a vestibule and a nave of ten bays, a large crossing with transepts, and a three-bay chancel. In plan, the chapel's vast footprint, longitudinal form, and buttresses assured that it was to be in keeping with the other collegiate Gothic buildings of Cross Campus. The chapel was conceived as a central element of Cross Campus, a foil to Sterling Memorial Library, and the representation of religion at the university center.

While the chapel was a pivotal element in the eyes of the university planners, the difficulty of bringing the chapel plans to reality revealed a greater ambiguity of feeling toward religion at Yale. The controversy over compulsory chapel at Yale in the 1920s, which called into question the very role of religion on the campus, contributed to the apparent apathy to the new chapel. Rogers had positioned the chapel on Cross Campus to not only symbolize religion's importance in the university mission but also make the chapel a gathering place for the entire university. The abolishment of compulsory chapel in 1926 put in doubt the need for such a chapel. With religious worship now voluntary, the number of students expected to attend services was greatly reduced, making the investment in a new chapel structure appear unnecessary and Rogers's proposed five-thousand-seat capacity foolish.

President Angell and the Yale Corporation attempted to cast the abolishment of mandatory chapel in terms of saving religion, not abandoning it. Angell acknowledged that the ending of compulsory chapel suggested "the final secularizing of the college, its flouting of the clear words of its charter, its desertion of the old loyalties, and its definite commitment to the mammon of unrighteousness." Still, he argued, "the true interests of religion would be more effectively promoted if . . . men were left to decide for themselves in what way they would express their religious interests."[50] To counter the appearance that the ending of compulsory chapel also meant the secularization of Yale, Angell advanced the prospect of a new chapel as an example of how Yale would preserve religion. He intimated that with the compulsory requirement gone, "voluntary services, particularly if a beautiful chapel can be secured for them," along with other measures to support religion "will promote a finer religious attitude on the part of the undergraduates, and more than compensate them for the loss of the ancient tradition of compulsory worship."[51] Yet however much Angell and Yale's planners believed in the importance of a new chapel, especially in the post–compulsory worship climate, the chapel plans were to languish and ultimately fade. While donors like John Sterling, Edward Harkness, and John D. Rockefeller were funneling massive amounts of money into other building projects at Yale, no donor appeared to fund the chapel project.

James Gamble Rogers, frustrated over the apparent end to the chapel project, remained adamant that the new heart of the Yale campus should include some presence of religion. If a new chapel was not to be located at this important site, something else signifying religion needed to be. The new Yale Divinity School could be an appropriate substitute. Just as Yale's other professional schools were expanding and jostling to position their new buildings in Yale's new campus plan, the Divinity School in the 1920s gathered enough funds to move from its old Gothic revival quadrangle north of Old Campus and build the new Sterling Divinity Quadrangle, designed by the architectural firm Delano and Aldrich. Rogers agreed with John Farwell, chairman of the Architectural Plan Committee, that positioning the Divinity School quadrangle opposite the new Sterling Memorial Library would "indicate the spiritual center of the university in balance with the library, at the other end of the Cross campus, expressing the intellectual center." Rogers said, "Of course, I never have given up the belief that a chapel should be in the center of our university," but he felt that "the divinity school very prominently located would express at least in a minor way that there existed in our university a little, anyhow, even if not enough of the spiritual side of our life."[52]

Yet the new Divinity School was ultimately constructed nearly a mile away from the campus center, and a new chapel would also never find its way onto Cross Campus. Their absence from the center also left Yale's central quadrangle incomplete. Instead of engaging in a conversation with a new chapel or divinity school, the Sterling Memorial Library looks blankly to the opposite end of the Cross Campus axis toward Franklin Hall (1910), a red brick, Georgian revival building that is neither aligned with the library nor in keeping with the collegiate Gothic character of Cross Campus. For Rogers, an appropriate spiritual expression would have to come in a more unconventional form. With no chapel or divinity school to balance the library, the Sterling Memorial Library, designed in the language of a cathedral and filled with religious images, itself fulfilled the spiritual role at Yale's center. Though the library arguably presented an even greater symbol of the university ideal by fusing knowledge and spirituality, it nevertheless signaled the decline of traditional religious forms and traditional worship at the center of Yale.

CHAPTER 4

NEW CATHEDRALS
FOR THE MODERN
UNIVERSITY

Among the attempts to retain an architectural presence of religion on campus,
the interwar decades saw a more inventive melding of religion into the
university's everyday work. At the University of Pittsburgh and Yale
University, a skyscraper classroom and a library became new kinds of
cathedrals on the campus. These buildings crafted a generically religious environment, rooted in neo-Gothic imagery, as a background to
university life, learning, and research.

The use of ecclesiastical forms for other purposes on campus was
not new. In the 1870s, the Victorian Gothic Memorial Hall by Ware
and Van Brunt at Harvard University employed the form of a church
in a building that housed a memorial, dining room, and auditorium.
William Appleton Potter's Victorian Gothic designs for the Chancellor
Green Library at Princeton and the Robinson Library at Brown University, both completed in the 1870s, also aligned religion and learning.
These late-nineteenth-century buildings were early examples of a fusion
of sacred and secular functions on campus, which Victorian Gothic architecture precisely captured.

Yet such religious imagery was distinct from that employed in the twentieth century. While the Victorian Gothic could communicate the easy relationship between religion and learning in the late nineteenth century, by the twentieth century this relationship on the American campus was more complicated. The use of the neo-Gothic in the twentieth century—now in more muted tones than the polychromatic Victorian Gothic and in more historically accurate forms—confronted a more complex picture. On the one hand, the neo-Gothic architecture of the University of Pittsburgh's Cathedral of Learning and Yale's Sterling Memorial Library fit within the broader architectural programs on these campuses. More convincingly, however, their architecture and iconography, along with the stated beliefs of the university leaders who oversaw them and the architects who designed them, argue for an ecclesiastical metaphor that attempted to reframe religion for the modern university in an attempt to save its presence on campus. These quasi-religious buildings—architecture that trafficked in religious imagery while housing other functions—became the new cathedrals on the modern American campus. As mandatory chapel policies were ended and traditional religious services were no longer part of the corporate life on campus, university leaders found alternative ways to assert religion into students' daily experience. Such double-coded imagery also allowed for the religious references to remain in the background, surpassed by scientific and modern concerns.

THE CATHEDRAL OF LEARNING
AT THE UNIVERSITY OF PITTSBURGH

In the 1930s, the University of Pittsburgh constructed a traditional chapel at the center of its campus (fig. 4.1). Funded by the Heinz family, the 450-seat nondenominational though clearly Christian Heinz Memorial Chapel (1934–38) put forward an image of religion on the campus deeply rooted in neo-Gothic imagery. University of Pittsburgh chancellor John Gabbert Bowman argued that future generations would "respond to its feeling-tones, to its organ tones, and the rest, and become freshly aware that we are moving toward life of good will and

Figure 4.1. View of the Heinz Memorial Chapel (left) and the Cathedral of Learning (right), University of Pittsburgh, by the architect Charles Klauder. University of Pittsburgh Historic Photographs, 1884–present, University Library System, University of Pittsburgh.

toward a living experience of God," echoing the emotional draw of such architecture that Reverend Herbert Parrish had found in the Princeton University Chapel.[1] The physical existence of the chapel building, irrespective of whether a student entered its doors, was to simply serve "by its presence" as a reminder of spiritual life on campus.[2] Like other university leaders, Chancellor Bowman believed religion had a necessary place in the education of American youth, and the chapel was intended to overtly signal these values to University of Pittsburgh students.

Yet on the University of Pittsburgh campus, there stood another building that literally and figuratively overshadowed the chapel (see fig. 4.1). Looming over the chapel across a 110-yard green was the transformative symbol of religion and modernity: the Cathedral of Learning, a forty-two-story Art Deco classroom building clothed in the imagery of the Gothic. The Cathedral of Learning dominated the university skyline and captured the imagination. It became the more important purveyor of the idea of religion in the modern American university, a new kind of worship space that infused a sense of reverence and spirituality into everyday learning and research. In this sense, the Cathedral of Learning effectively reconciled empirical and revealed knowledge. But ultimately, in creating a generic spiritual environment within a skyscraper form, the Cathedral of Learning placed religion in the background of the modernity it sought to recognize. While Chancellor Bowman had an optimistic view on this transformation of the material expression of religion on campus, it nevertheless allowed religion to be surpassed by other concerns.

Bowman inherited an institution underfunded and overcrowded when he became chancellor of the University of Pittsburgh, then a private, nondenominational institution, in 1921.[3] The university faced a debt of over $1 million and an unbalanced operating budget.[4] From 1916 to 1923, the university's student population had nearly doubled, from about 4,000 to 7,800.[5] By the 1920s, students were elbow to elbow in a borrowed library space. The university's four primary buildings and even the temporary buildings constructed during World War I failed to meet basic needs, forcing some classes to be held outside in fair weather.[6] To solve this crisis, Chancellor Bowman convinced Andrew and Richard Mellon to pay the university's debts, and he imagined a skyscraper classroom arising at the center of campus.[7]

For Bowman, the skyscraper classroom was to meet two clear and complementary aims: to express that the University of Pittsburgh was a modern institution, dedicated to the excitement and advances of a scientific age, and an institution still devoted to the spiritual dimension of education. Bowman did not see these as contradictory aims, and he sought an architectural form that would meld them together. Edward Purcell Mellon, the Mellons' nephew and the first architect hired to design the new development on what was called Frick Acres, produced a scheme in 1923 that followed the Oxbridge model, complete with irregular quadrangles, Gothic styling, and a curious polygonal Gothic tower as the centerpiece. But Bowman rejected this Oxbridge-heavy plan, saying that Oxford University buildings "interpret an era that is gone." Bowman was searching instead for a design to "express its age—an age of creative, forceful energy directed toward usefulness."[8] That age in education was dominated by empirical knowledge, knowledge that to Bowman was changing the world:

> We live, however, in a new age; in an age that lies open for action. Science, for example, is no longer merely a receptive process of recognizing truth. It is a live thing, intent upon a creative, imaginative application of knowledge to human use. Transportation, steel, and power, as we know them today, are results of this, as are the aeroplane, the radio, and the Diesel engine. In medicine, chemistry, and biology, the same creative spirit has led to discoveries comparable to the discovery of a new continent. In the social sciences, again, the same process goes on, though less obviously, broadening our outlook and dispelling sentimental theories.[9]

But religion, spirituality, and moral values were not to be discounted in this scientific, progressive age. Bowman defined the spirit of the University of Pittsburgh as aligning with the virtues of intelligence, courage, and spiritual fineness, and he believed that the desired skyscraper tower, while not "[producing] in us courage, daring, or reverence [or] mak[ing] us 'good' would nevertheless activate those qualities." Bowman believed such a skyscraper would "stimulate a sort of kinetic and exalted thinking on the part of students and faculty."[10] In imagining that architecture could symbolize a creative power alongside "exalted" thinking, Bowman was crafting a way to embrace science while bringing religion into the modern age.

The fifty-two-story building that the newly hired architect Charles Klauder delivered in his initial concept in 1924—and realized in forty-two stories—achieved just this combination. It was a modern skyscraper, influenced by the 1922 Chicago Tribune Tower competition

and the Art Deco tenets of a setback tower and uninterrupted vertical lines. In form, the Cathedral of Learning captured the vitality and
spirituality Bowman desired. Klauder created a cathedral skyscraper
that appeared to be forever reaching higher. Out of a low-lying base
emerged a series of flat-roofed pseudo-buttresses of varying heights
clustered around the tallest tower. These symbolic buttresses recalled
the traditional forms of a Gothic cathedral without replicating their
original structural purpose. Uninterrupted vertical lines on these at-
tenuated forms emphasized the building's height, and multistory lancet
arches organized tall banks of windows. The sole horizontal features
of the building were the pseudo-buttresses' flat-topped roofs. Bowman, remarkable for his ability to connect ideals to their architectural
manifestations, articulated what the unabashed vertical thrust of the
skyscraper was to symbolize: "Force, daring, courage, achievement,
all are there. Not measured, yet visible, greatness rises before us. The
imagination starts. A rush of self-expansion comes and a feeling that
we can go beyond our own limits."[11] The Cathedral of Learning captured the modern zeitgeist.

If these elements of verticality expressed the excitement of the
modern age and the possibilities of knowledge and science, the building's ornament spoke to the spiritual dimension of education. These
Gothic elements signaled the building's educational identity. To counter
the supposition that a tall building necessarily signified "commerce,
competition, and contest," Bowman explained that the building included ecclesiastical references to prove it fostered a "college life which
has an indomitable spiritual value in it."[12] Pointed arch windows, tre-
foils and quatrefoils, and tracery adorned the building at select points.
The "spiritual quality" of the building resided in these details, whose
archetypal associations linked them with religious architecture. "At
each corner of the tower, conspicuous by its position, occurs Gothic
ornamentation," said Bowman. "The character of this ornamentation,
here in contrast to the otherwise stern simplicity of the building, means
to us, through association with church buildings, a mood of worship
and reverence."[13] An undated drawing compares the elevation of the
Cathedral of Learning to those of the Notre Dame and Reims Cathedrals in France and the unfinished tower of Malines in Belgium, un-

derscoring its religious and Gothic allusions. Klauder's design melded a sense of invigoration, rushing forward, and limitless discovery with a spiritual sense underpinning these advances, thereby reconciling the modern and religious pursuits of the university.

The interior of the Cathedral of Learning furthers this appropriation of religious imagery. To again underscore the place of spirituality in education, the Commons Room on the building's main floor presented an image of a Gothic nave (fig. 4.2).[14] The room, which Bowman called "the heart and soul of the building," was to produce the same effect as a church. "Put into the stone arches the spirituality that belongs with education," Bowman reportedly instructed Klauder. "Draw a room that will so grip a boy that he will never enter it with his hat on."[15] The 175-by-128-foot room, made of Indiana limestone, possessed the hallmark forms of a Gothic cathedral: cluster columns, webbed vaults, more pointed arches, and stone tracery and ornament. At three stories tall, belying the mass over it, the room also recalled the height of a cathedral nave. Guastavino tile vaulting hushes sounds within the half-acre space, inducing a reverential demeanor in those who enter. Heavy oak furniture possesses a medieval and even religious intimation. Against the stone piers are groupings of three chairs, one larger than the others with a high wood back suggesting a bishop's chair. An iron gate by Samuel Yellin proclaims to the students studying and meeting in the room, "Here Is Eternal Spring for You the Very Stars of Heaven Are New." And if students needed an even more explicit religious symbolism, on the higher floors of the Cathedral of Learning the pointed Gothic windows assert a religious presence in the workaday life of the university.[16]

In referencing the spiritual and the modern, the empirical and the revealed, the building was to "give unity to the whole idea of education" by bringing together the concepts of empirical and revealed knowledge. The Cathedral of Learning hosted the three-story university library, classrooms, laboratories, and research space, in addition to faculty and departmental offices. In total, the skyscraper contained some 750 rooms by 1937. Whereas separate buildings give students the "idea that these subjects are separate things and unrelated just as the buildings are," Bowman believed "the high building would give unity to the

Figure 4.2. Commons Room, Cathedral of Learning. University of Pittsburgh Historic Photographs, 1884–present, University Library System, University of Pittsburgh.

entire university."[17] The discoveries made in the scientific laboratories, the knowledge gained in the library, and information received in the lecture halls were enveloped in a spiritual environment. A sense of reverence, worship, and spirituality governed all work that went on in the building. More than unifying the various parts of the modern university, the Cathedral of Learning was to unify the knowledge gained from science and from religion.

The building's very name, the Cathedral of Learning, was an assertion of this intent. Although Bowman initially expressed his displeasure at the name, he came to embrace it, especially for its "great publicity value," which was crucial to the ambitious public fund-raising campaign to pay for its construction.[18] More important, the name promoted the spiritual identity of the skyscraper, transforming it from a commercial-type building into one with a higher purpose.[19] The name called attention to the building's Gothic ornamentation and height and suggested its identity as a new kind of cathedral for the university, one that assumed the prominence and centrality typical of a Gothic cathedral. As Bowman explained its meaning, "This name is suggested partly by the Gothic architecture and partly by the idea that the 'cathedral' is to be a *seat* or central symbol of creativeness and achievement in the Pittsburgh district."[20] The appropriation of a religious name for the building signaled the idea that university education was affiliated with spiritual ideals.

Not everyone understood this melding. The pastor of the nearby First Baptist Church, Dr. Carl Wallace Petty, agreed with Bowman that the Heinz Memorial Chapel and the Cathedral of Learning exemplified the unity of knowledge but argued that empirical and revealed knowledge were divided between the two. "Chapel of Prayer and Cathedral of Learning—religion and science—altar and laboratory—faith and reason, these it seems God hath joined together," Petty said. "We follow our highest institution and truest experience when in the heart of our city we place these two temples side by side."[21] Dr. Henry Sloane Coffin, the Presbyterian minister who spoke at the dedication of the Heinz Memorial Chapel, also differentiated the functions of the two structures in saying it was "appropriate" that a university "would have a chapel for religious worship side by side with its towering building devoted to other tasks."[22]

These ministers missed the real transformative meaning that the Cathedral of Learning came to have. As the iconic and dominant building at the University of Pittsburgh, literally overshadowing the chapel, it was the Cathedral of Learning—not the chapel—that was the university's primary purveyor of spirituality. A striking photograph evinces this shift. Taken in the 1950s during the Christmas season, the photograph shows the image of an illuminated cross in the upper windows of the Cathedral of Learning (fig. 4.3). The image proclaims religion's significance within the university and in the Pittsburgh skyline. It was a new cathedral, seeking to integrate religion in the modern era.

THE STERLING MEMORIAL LIBRARY AT YALE UNIVERSITY

In the 1930s, Yale University also constructed a new kind of cathedral at its campus center (fig. 4.4). James Gamble Rogers, who oversaw the remaking of the Yale campus in the 1920s and 1930s, long believed that the center of Yale's campus needed to have a religious expression. When plans for both a new chapel and a divinity school at the campus center were abandoned, Rogers preserved religion, or at least a version of it, at the Yale center by creating a new sacred space for the modern American university—a cathedral library laden with religious iconography (fig. 4.5).[23]

The overt religious imagery of the Sterling Memorial Library was immediately recognized. In 1931, less than three weeks after its dedication, Yale senior and future journalist, William Harlan Hale, gave a vivid and scathing account of the library's religious image in an article descriptively titled "Yale's Cathedral Orgy":

> A library? You would never recognize it when you saw it. Enter it—pass through a bastard version of the west portal of an abbey. Continue down the main hall, which is a precise copy of a nave with

Figure 4.3. Cathedral of Learning at Christmas with the image of a cross illuminated in its windows. The spire of the Heinz Memorial Chapel is evident at left. University of Pittsburgh Historic Photographs, 1884–present, University Library System, University of Pittsburgh.

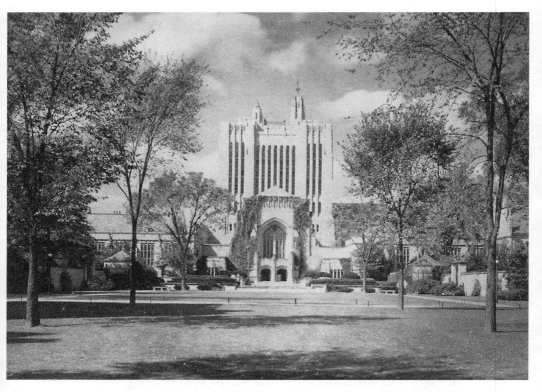

Figure 4.4. Sterling Memorial Library, Yale University, James Gamble Rogers, 1927–31, pictured in the late 1930s. From RU 696, Manuscripts and Archives, Yale University Library.

five bays. Observe the massive and unnecessary piers, the inconvenient but orthodox side aisles, the lofty transepts bristling with sanctity above and serial catalogues below. Advance to the high altar—a $25,000 book-delivery desk; overhead, admire the rood screen, of utmost complexity and facility at catching dust, which has been cleverly placed to hide the important library clock from view. . . . Turn about and gaze at the triforium gallery above the vast nave; scan the splendid clerestory windows, heavy with tracery and mullions, highly effective in minimizing the light, and sealed hermetically shut. Pass down the corridors, and cry out in rapt adoration of more color,

Figure 4.5. Entrance hall, Sterling Memorial Library. From RU 696, Manuscripts and Archives, Yale University Library.

more carving, more corbels, more plaques, balconies, chandeliers, wall brackets (electric, in the style of ancient torch-holders), more sacred splendors! And, while at last laboring to find a book, bow your head in holy ecstasy![24]

Hale saw the Sterling Memorial Library as an affront to modern life. Its architecture was not even a neutral background; it was an active negative agent subverting the very aims of the library. Playing off Yale's motto, *Lux et Veritas*, Light and Truth, Hale famously remarked elsewhere, "There is not one suggestion of *Veritas* in the Sterling Library;— and for that matter there is a precious little of *Lux*."[25] Moreover, the building seemingly denied the modern knowledge produced and consumed within its walls. "A modern building constructed for purely modern needs," he scolded, "has no excuse for going off in an orgy of meretricious medievalism and stale iconography."[26]

Hale condemned the library's architectural revivalism in the interest of promoting modern architecture, a movement that would gain widespread attention in the Museum of Modern Art's 1932 *Modern Architecture: An International Exhibition* just one year after Hale's biting review. But for Yale's leaders and the library's architect, James Gamble Rogers, the significance of constructing a library in the image of a Gothic cathedral overrode any desire to employ avant-garde architecture. At the library's dedication, Yale president James Rowland Angell articulated the building's ecclesiastical metaphor as a "temple of the mind" to protect the eternal "sacred lamp of learning" and the "holy torch of truth." Most powerfully, Angell proclaimed, "Here is incarnate the intellectual and spiritual life of Yale."[27] These carefully chosen words, combined with the library's neo-Gothic imagery, asserted that learning and truth possessed an everlasting connection to the divine even for those library patrons whose subject was scientific, whose research approach was empirical, or whose work otherwise appeared to have little connection with religious concerns.

By the interwar years in the twentieth century, religion faced an uncertain future on Yale's campus. It was no longer a dominant focus of academic inquiry, challenged by the emerging religious plurality of the student body, and yet still a desired component in students' moral formation. The Sterling Memorial Library emerged at this crossroad in the making of the modern Yale. If religion could no longer be the central aim of higher education, it nevertheless could form the backdrop to all university work, a reminder of the ultimate aim of all human inquiry. In casting the pursuit of knowledge in a religious image, the Sterling Memorial Library became library *and* cathedral.

Yet however genuinely the Yale administration and Rogers believed that the cathedral library successfully preserved a place for religion in the modern university, the library's ecclesiastical metaphor, embodied in its cathedral organization, Virgin Mary–like "altar piece," and Gutenberg Bible relic, allowed multiple interpretations. For some, it reaffirmed religion's role amidst great change in higher education. For others, it mocked religion, confirming that religion belonged to a past no longer relevant to modern life. William Harlan Hale's irreverent marrying of "cathedral" and "orgy" attests to the growing ascendancy of secular over religious life. These divergent views of the Sterling Memorial Library reflect religion's tenuous position in higher education in the twentieth century.

Library as Skyscraper and Cathedral

The Sterling Memorial Library's organization reveals Rogers's attempt to meld multiple identities within one structure and acknowledge the tensions at work in the modern university: revealed and empirical, old and new, traditional and modern, conservative and progressive, divine and human. Yale University librarian Andrew Keogh identified such tensions when he stated the building was "as efficient as an up-to-date factory and as beautiful as a cathedral."[28] Wilhelm Munthe, a Norwegian librarian commenting in the 1930s, called the library "a combination of skyscraper, cathedral, and cloister."[29] These descriptions focused on the two outstanding features of the large library complex: the modern book stack tower and the ecclesiastical entrance sequence. These distinctive spaces both mirrored the tensions of the modern university and attempted to reconcile them.

The library's book stack tower, first proposed by Bertram Grosvenor Goodhue in his original designs of the library and retained by

Rogers when he took over the design after Goodhue's death in 1924, celebrated rather than hid the stacks. At sixteen stories and 150 feet tall, the tower was a "book skyscraper," the library's most modern element.[30] Goodhue and Rogers drew on other architectural precedents to create this skyscraper library. The vertical organization of the tower's windows recalled Goodhue's entry in the 1922 Chicago Tribune Tower competition, which Rogers had also entered, as well as Goodhue's design for the Nebraska State Capitol.[31] In addition to playing off the modern zeitgeist typified by the American skyscraper, the library tower became a leitmotif in collegiate architecture as universities struggled to house increasing numbers of books and collections. Klauder's Cathedral of Learning (1924–37) at the University of Pittsburgh, G. G. Scott's Cambridge University Library (1931–34), Henry van de Velde's book tower (1933) at Ghent University, and Paul Cret's University of Texas tower (1937) also employed the skyscraper model, although with different stylistic effects, as an innovative solution to accommodating the products of modern knowledge.[32]

The Sterling Memorial Library's medieval stone cladding and picturesque roofline belied the rational, modern structure underneath. Hale relayed the story of a "well-known modern Swedish architect" who was crestfallen while visiting the university when he learned that the tower of steel girders, which he proclaimed as "something really modern at Yale," was to be covered with stone instead of glass.[33] Hale published a photograph of the book stack tower under construction in the *Harkness Hoot* as an example of what modern architecture at Yale could be: structure frankly expressed, with little ornamentation and certainly no historicizing cladding. Above his juxtaposition of this photograph to an image of the completed library was the mournful headline, "IT MIGHT HAVE BEEN."[34]

The book stack tower further symbolized the ascendancy of the laboratory in the modern university. As one description stated, "The library is a working laboratory in the true sense of the word, and the bookstack tower is the heart of the structure, bringing readers and books quickly and easily together."[35] The tower housed three hundred study carrels as well as seminar rooms for students to discover, analyze, and invent in close proximity to their research subjects, and elevators and pneumatic tubes carried materials from the tower to the delivery desk. The tower epitomized the production of new knowledge that the modern university had come to embody.

From this perspective, the symbolism the stacks carried was not of ages past but rather of knowledge's relation to modern life. Munthe asserted that the tower "overlooks the town as a symbol that the book is a power-factor in modern society."[36] At the center of Cross Campus, elevated for all to see, the vast store of human knowledge was celebrated. For the British librarian and sometime-playwright Louis Stanley Jast, the stacks rose above the messiness of modern life to proclaim humanity's collective knowledge: "Then hail! / Thou mighty pile of books, thou glorious thrust / Of learning above moil and rage and dust, / Wisdom's uplifted finger, soul of Yale!"[37]

For all its external expressiveness, the book stack tower finds little acknowledgment in the library's interior; students reach the stacks by an inconspicuous elevator to the side of the delivery desk. Rather, the overwhelming experience of the interior is the sensory experience of library-cum-cathedral that William Harlan Hale's description so vividly re-creates. Rogers cunningly adapted the organization of a cathedral to the purposes of the library. The book stack tower visually recedes as the library patron approaches what Hale termed the "bastard abbey portal" in the library's smaller entrance tower on the Cross Campus lawn. From this dim, compressed entrance defined by arches and heavy carvings, students, faculty, and visitors are released into the neo-Gothic glory of the library's entrance hall. The walls of the soaring, five-bay nave, formed by robust stone columns supporting pointed arches, follow the customary cathedral division of arcade, triforium, and clerestory. The crossing and transepts complete the familiar ecclesiastical pattern, and the nearby cloister and courtyard suggest a monastic compound. Although hushed voices within a library are common, here the reason for a reverential demeanor has another dimension—a religious one. As *Scientific American* described it, "The Gothic architecture adapted to library needs gives a feeling of spaciousness and calm which has an excellent psychological effect."[38]

Although the Sterling Memorial Library first appears as a cathedral, closer inspection reveals curious substitutions. In the narthex, telephone booths are disguised as confessionals. Card catalogs nestled underneath the side aisles stand in place of pews. At the head of the entrance nave under fan vaulting, an elaborately carved oak delivery desk is in place of the altar. The reading room off the transept is in the image of a refectory, and the rare book room emulates a lady chapel.[39] The Librarian's Courtyard (now Selin Courtyard) recalls a monastic courtyard, complete with a central fountain in the manner of the monastic washing basin. Rogers had, in effect, placed the functions of a modern library within the shell of a neo-Gothic cathedral.

Descriptions of the library in the *Yale University Library Gazette* asserted that attempts were made to mitigate such ecclesiastical overtones: "[The library] avoids too churchlike a character through the introduction of leaded glass in which colour is largely supplanted by intricate patterning in leadwork," and "a painted wood ceiling of rather simple design helps to preserve a secular character."[40] Evidence to the contrary, however, overwhelmed this claim. Contemporary accounts, such as the one in the *Harvard Crimson* describing the library as having a "magnificent cathedral-like edifice," immediately picked up on the religious allusion.[41] William Harlan Hale's fury underscored that the library enthusiastically embraced the ecclesiastical metaphor to the point of sacrificing practicality.

Alma Mater as Virgin Mary

The climax of the Sterling Memorial Library's cathedral orgy is the *Alma Mater* mural at the culmination of the entrance nave (fig. 4.6). Painted by Eugene Francis Savage, a Yale professor of fine arts, and installed in 1933, two years after the library's dedication, the mural is a religious allusion so strong it would have added considerably more fuel to Hale's fire had it been finished before the publication of his "Yale's Cathedral Orgy."[42] Echoing President Angell's assertion that the library embodied "the intellectual and spiritual life of Yale,"[43] Savage envisioned his mural as symbolizing "the inspiration that directs the University's spiritual and intellectual efforts."[44] The *Alma Mater* mural, which the *Harkness Hoot* derisively deemed "the ideal altar-piece for a building which is in every respect also an absurd travesty of the Gothic style," plays with its overt

Figure 4.6. The *Alma Mater* mural (1933) by Eugene Savage in its location above the delivery desk in Sterling Memorial Library. From RU 696, Manuscripts and Archives, Yale University Library.

religious iconography, fusing together ecclesiastical forms and secular content to allow a double-coded meaning.[45] This mural, working in concert with its complementary neo-Gothic architecture, is a key component to understanding the library as a complete representation of a Gothic cathedral and a total work of art.

In the mural, positioned above the library's delivery desk, pulled curtains reveal the female figure of Yale's Alma Mater standing frontally. A blue and white mantel covers her white Grecian garment, and a laurel wreath crowns her head. Engaging the viewer with her direct stare, she stands in front of the Tree of Knowledge under a trilobed arch, supported by Corinthian columns and adorned with the towers of a vaguely medieval city. She holds a book in her right hand inscribed with Yale's motto, *Lux et Veritas*, in Hebrew letters and the sphere of learning in her left.

Savage gave physical form to Yale's motto in two female figures at the left of the mural. Light, bearing a torch and adorned with a crown of light rays, and Truth, naked, holding a mirror and crowned with a halo, bring the six male figures of Music, Divinity, Fine Arts, Literature, Science, and Labor "to make grateful acknowledgement to Alma Mater." Each subject of knowledge and human endeavor is represented with its appropriate attributes. Divinity is garbed in a cross-covered robe and signaled with a halo. Literature is robed, with a laurel wreath crown, a quill pen and paper in hand, and hand over heart as if to give an oration. Music bows down to Alma Mater with harp in hand, while Fine Arts, clothed in a painter's smock and holding a palette, lays a figure of Winged Victory at the feet of Alma Mater. At Alma Mater's left, separated from the others, Science holds a microscope, and Labor, grasping a hammer and sickle, presents the fruits of the earth to Alma Mater.[46]

The work is in many respects a very proper, straightforward allegorical mural celebrating the work of the university. The figure of Alma Mater personifies Yale. The blue and white colors of her clothing mirror the colors of the university. Her book displays the Yale motto, which is also embodied in the figures of Light and Truth. Laurel wreaths and Corinthian columns signify wisdom, and the sphere of learning represents the realms of learning available in the university. The Winged Victory statue, an imitation of the famed Greek Winged

Victory of Samothrace, symbolizes truth's victory over evil, and the fruits of the earth suggest an understanding and harvesting of the physical world. The mural articulates both the university's role in gathering knowledge and the higher ideals that govern that acquisition.

But like almost everything else in the Sterling Memorial Library, the mural also possesses a strong religious connotation. The immediate impression of the mural is of a religious icon. Alma Mater reads as the Virgin Mary or at least a saint; the blue in her garments is a classic Marian depiction, and the white signifies sainthood. Formally, the composition itself makes divine references. The trilobed arch above Alma Mater rings her head as if it were a halo, echoing the halos of Truth at the left and Divinity at the right. The three arcs within the arch evoke the Holy Trinity, as does the triangular, symmetrical arrangement of the three haloed figures of Alma Mater, Truth, and Divinity. The Tree of Knowledge, taken from the Book of Genesis, represents the knowledge of good and evil, and the medieval city suggests heavenly Jerusalem. If the mural is a representation of the university's role in producing knowledge, it is equally a representation of knowledge's divine origin.

The architecture of the library heightens the mural's religious associations. Positioned at the culmination of the entrance nave, above the "altar" and rood screen of the delivery desk, under fan vaults, and within a pointed arch, the painting appears as an altarpiece. The inscription on the extravagantly carved oak delivery desk, "Many shall run to and fro, and knowledge shall be increased" (Daniel 12:4), from the Old Testament Book of Daniel, strengthens the religious association. As a modern, sophisticated equipment system of conveyor belts and pneumatic tubes worked behind the desk to deliver items from across the library, above the desk Alma Mater, appearing as a religious figure, guards, governs, and oversees access to the immense store of knowledge in the book stack tower beyond.[47]

Within the Sterling Memorial Library, the *Alma Mater* mural combined with the library's procession made palpable knowledge's divine association. Entering through the bastard abbey portal, walking past the telephone-booth confessionals, visiting the card catalog in the side aisle, and processing to the circulation desk altar to present a book request under the gaze of Alma Mater was a ritual experience with intentional religious overtones. Such visual and bodily cues indicate to the library patron religion's authority and relevance to the work ahead. As Sally Promey argued in her analysis of John Singer Sargent's *Triumph of Religion* murals in the Boston Public Library, the ritual purpose of Sargent Hall is an "orchestrated preparation for privileged intellectual activity."[48] The entrance hall of the Sterling Memorial Library similarly orchestrates a sense of knowledge's divine origin before a student or faculty member enters the reading room or ascends the stacks. As Rogers wrote, the "large and imposing" entrance hall was intended "to give the best first impression and the best last impression."[49] The *Alma Mater* mural intensifies this experience. Although the mural may be read as an allegorical representation of the university, the decided impression it gives is as an altarpiece for a cathedral library, albeit a shocking one for a historically Protestant institution.

Religious and Secular Iconography

In mixing secular and religious content, the Sterling Memorial Library's rich iconographic program fosters and reinforces multiple interpretations of the building's meaning. That its trustees sacrificed six tiers of book stacks in order to fund more ornament indicates the importance they assigned to the symbolic expression of the library.[50] Yale professors aided in the selection of the images and inscriptions, and a 1931 issue of the *Yale University Library Gazette* meticulously, even ponderously, recorded the sources of the decorations.[51] For example, the entry for a Cro-Magnon image in the library reads, "Wall engraving of a bison and horse from Les Combarelles. Second phase. Aurignacian epoch."[52] Such detail and classification reflected the mastery of modern scholarship and promoted the library's role in preserving knowledge.

Embedded in the neo-Gothic shell are images and words that variously describe the history of recorded knowledge, the history of Yale, and the tie between religion and knowledge. At the library's main entrance, a medieval scholar divides the portal, above which are carved a Mayan serpent, an Athenian owl, and a Roman wolf representing the European and American civilizations and Greek and Arabic inscriptions signifying the ancient. In the fan vaults over the delivery desk, carvings of record-keeping implements range from the ancient chisel and hammer, sand shaker, and quill pen and scroll to the modern typewriter keyboard, telegraph key, and telephone.[53] Images of the previous Yale library buildings surmount the York Street entryway, and ten triforium panels in the entrance hall record scenes from the history of the Yale library, including the founding of Yale College. Words also reinforce the connection between religion and learning. The inscription over the door of the librarian's office from Shakespeare's *Henry VI* offers this moralizing message: "Ignorance is the curse of God / Knowledge the wing wherewith we fly to heaven."[54] An Arabic inscription taken from the Koran over the library entrance reads, "God! There is no God but he . . . He knoweth that which is past, and that which is to come unto them, and they shall not comprehend anything of his knowledge, but so far as he pleaseth."[55]

And, as is often cited in descriptions of the Sterling Memorial Library, some images challenge the library's rarefied atmosphere. A bookworm in different stages of development enlivens the lanterns on the library's Wall Street entrance, and lest the purpose of the janitor's closet on the first floor across from the altar-like circulation desk be misinterpreted, inscribed within two very proper looking shields over the door are a mop and bucket and brooms.[56] A figure carved on a corbel studiously hunched over a book whose pages read, "U R A JOKE," greets the visitor walking through the cloistered exhibition corridor.[57] Such unexpected cheekiness within ecclesiastical forms challenges the expectations drawn from the library's architecture, opening up the possibility for new readings and allowing the building to be both a nod to a religious past and a modern, secular present.

Within this varied iconography, so dense that William Harlan Hale cautioned that it was "meaningless without a handbook," is a dual reading of Johannes Gutenberg and his invention that particularly strikes the traditional and modern, revealed and empirical, divine and human tensions the library embodies.[58] Like the *Alma Mater* mural, the display of Yale's copy of the Gutenberg Bible exemplified the fluidity in meaning the library as a whole fosters.[59] As a document of the Word of God, the Gutenberg Bible is the very definition of revealed knowledge: its passages contain messages from God, recount the life of Christ, and instruct how one should live a moral life. Within the Sterling Memorial Library, the Gutenberg Bible was presented as a religious relic. At the end of the rare book room, positioned symbolically at the front of the library on Cross Campus, was, as one observer exclaimed, "a chapel in the corner for the Gutenberg Bible!"[60] James Gamble Rogers had indeed created a chapel-like space, a polygonal chamber set off by iron gates by Samuel Yellin, whose tall walls, pierced by lancet windows, culminate in fan vaults. Originally the Gutenberg Bible was placed at the center of this "Grand Exhibition Room," displayed and protected under glass. Movement through the library to see the Bible in this protected environment created a secondary ritualistic event akin to a pilgrimage to venerate a relic. This reading of the Gutenberg Bible as a sacred object supported the interpretation of the Sterling Memorial Library as a sacred space, overtly Christian in tone and message.

Yet another, nonreligious reading of the Bible and its setting was possible. Made by German printer Johannes Gutenberg beginning in 1455 with his printing press, the Gutenberg Bible marked an early use of movable type, a revolution in printing and bookmaking that allowed for the mass production of books. Aside from its religious content, the Bible is an extraordinarily important document of the beginning of the modern transmission of knowledge. It was in this sense also a secular relic. Its guarded display in the library's rare book room signaled its historical value and significance, especially to a library filled with the products of Gutenberg's invention.

The depiction of Gutenberg and his printing press in the library's courtyard further stressed the fine line between the secular and religious interpretations of the Gutenberg Bible. The theme of the Librarians' Courtyard, landscaped by Beatrix Jones Farrand and itself a monastic-like space, paid homage to printing and the graphic arts. At the southeast entrance to the courtyard is an image of the Gutenberg press and below a pair of shields, one with the head of Gutenberg and the other an open book with the inscription, "In the beginning was the Word."[61] These suggest that Gutenberg and his invention heralded the beginning of the large-scale production of the printed word and the start of modern knowledge. But for those who could recognize its source, the inscription was incomplete. In full, the first verse from the Gospel of John reads,

"In the beginning was the Word, and the Word was with God, and the Word was God" (John 1:1). The appropriation of the quote for Gutenberg, and the pairing of it with a relief of his image, suggests that modern knowledge—the entire range of human discovery shared with others through the printed word—possessed its own form of divinity. On the other hand, the quote's implicit religious source suggested this new knowledge's religious foundation and its sanctification.

Finally, the iconography at the very center of the library also directly engages this dual reading. Prominently displayed on the arch before the crossing of the entrance hall nave are eleven bosses taken from the *Speculum humanae salvationis*, a medieval manuscript presented to the school in 1715 by Elihu Yale, the patron who donated over four hundred books and gave financial support to the fledgling institution and after whom the university is named. The *Speculum*, translated as the "Mirror of Salvation," used both words and images to show that events from the Old Testament prefigured those in the New Testament. Former Yale secretary, Anson Phelps Stokes, suggested developing the theme of the mirror from this manuscript in the library's iconography "because the library reflects the world's knowledge."[62] Images were drawn from both the Old and New Testaments: Jonah and the whale, fishermen drawing in their nets, the fiery furnace, Daniel and the lions, the adoration of the Magi, the creation of Eve, David and the beasts, Noah, the Baptism in Jordan, and the flight into Egypt.[63] The arch culminates with a depiction of the Nativity, illustrating the beginning of man's salvation through Christ. These bosses reinforced Christianity as the path to salvation as library patrons passed underneath them in their procession to the delivery desk altar. From a strictly historical standpoint, however, these *Speculum* images highlight an important written source of religious instruction in the Middle Ages and pay homage to the university's namesake. Like much of the library's iconography, these images possess both sacred and secular interpretations.

Reception of Yale's Ecclesiastical Metaphor

The ecclesiastical metaphor and even irony of the Sterling Memorial Library was not lost on its contemporaries at its opening. The library's appropriation of religious imagery sat uncomfortably for some. One visitor described the library's edifice as similar to one "in my memory of an old illustrated Bible for children" but wondered, "Was it the Tower of Babel, or a Babylonian palace?"[64] This tongue-in-cheek rhetorical question identified the building as either a supreme example of human pride and direct challenge to God's authority—an act for which God, in the story of the Tower of Babel, punished humans by dividing their language, a story perhaps appropriate to a library and a university— or so beautiful as to be like one of the seven Wonders of the World. A cartoon in the *Yale Record* depicted the interior of the library's entrance nave with a student asking an irritated adult, "Say, when does the feature begin?"[65] The library, or rather Tower of Babel or movie palace, recalled multiple images of fantastic spaces.

For a writer in *Commonweal*, the most striking part of the library was the cathedral-like entrance hall with its confessional telephone booths and massive columns. Most astonishingly of all, "The altar is the place at which books are dispensed!" The author got to the heart of the library's significance to a modern university in which scientific pursuits had superseded religion as the primary concern: "Thinking the whole thing over, one is torn between a tendency to find the whole affair just slightly ridiculous and a feeling that is quite unintentionally symbolic. After all, is it not science (of every form and order) to which innumerable moderns bring sacrifice and from which they expect help and solace?"[66] Here, the writer astutely identified the tensions and transformations at work in the university. As much as the Sterling Memorial Library sought to keep religion central within the minds of the faculty and students of the modern American university, a deep shift had already occurred in which religion played a secondary role. Although the altar-like circulation desk dominated by the guise of Alma Mater cultivated a religious atmosphere, those seeking books from the skyscraper beyond nevertheless increasingly sought the substance of science, not religion.

Other critiques took advantage of the Sterling Memorial Library's iconography and architecture to frankly mock the earnestness of placing religion at the center of the university. A suggested replacement for Savage's *Alma Mater* mural from Yale's humor magazine presented an irreverent account of university life.[67] Whereas Savage sought to express the intellectual and spiritual life of Yale, the artist of this parody illustrated the sordid in student life, inserting alcohol bottles and dice into Savage's composition, just as the library inserted its own imagery into an ecclesiastical framework. The seemingly inebriated Alma Mater holding a mug of beer certainly contrasted with the pure image of a Mary figure in Savage's original. This parody is shockingly effective in its irreverence, precisely because the real *Alma Mater* mural reads so strongly as a religious image.

Another critique was a satiric defense of the library notably written in verse, in which the poet admitted that the "Library is anachronistic, / Revivalistic, mystic, and atavisitic." Yet the poet reasoned that the library's religious image was secondary to its function:

> I see no good reason why things pedagogical
> Should not be allied to things theological.
> If we are true Sons of Eli and bibliophiles,
> Such minor details ought not to stir our biles.
> A library's the place for intellectual concepts
> Whether it be round or square or have a nave and two transcepts.[68]

This poem ironically captured the Sterling Memorial Library's intended purpose: It was to be the omnipresent religious background for the modern work at hand. From the perspective of Yale's leaders and James Gamble Rogers, if religion was no longer the central concern of university education, it nevertheless retained a rightful role in the university. The library crafted a place for religion in modern inquiry by appealing to the liberal Protestant notion of the unity of truth.

The library's ecclesiastical metaphor reinforced the deeper origins and outcomes of every search for truth. In employing religious imagery in a building frequented by students, the Sterling Memorial Library also cunningly created a regular religious experience without compulsion while emphasizing the religious dimension of education—thus taking over and even improving the purpose of the defunct compulsory chapel requirement. As the central gathering space for Yale, with space to accommodate over two thousand students and scholars at any given time, the library subtly fulfilled the same communal role as compulsory chapel. Especially given the absence of a new chapel at the Yale center, the library's intention was to make all who entered its doors understand that all learning was sacred and the mission of the university in part religious.

The Sterling Memorial Library was not the first or only library on the American campus to appeal to the ecclesiastical metaphor. In addition to the antebellum libraries at Harvard and Yale, the Gothic revival persisted in such buildings as the William Rainey Harper Memorial Library (Shepley, Rutan, and Coolidge, 1912) at the University of Chicago; the Henry Suzzallo Library (Gould and Bebb, 1923–26) at the University of Washington in Seattle; and James Gamble Rogers's other neo-Gothic library, the Charles Deering Library (1931–33) at Northwestern University. Although perhaps the desire to signal adherence to the whole man theory of education was the principal reason behind the selection of the neo-Gothic for these libraries as well as for countless dormitories, dining halls, laboratories, and lecture halls, the widespread religious imagery on the American university campus in the early twentieth century also suggests an underlying attempt to reframe religion for the modern era.

This reshaping of religion is certainly true for the Sterling Memorial Library. Yet even as James Gamble Rogers and Yale's leaders intended it to negotiate an accord between religion and modern knowledge at the heart of the university, much like the Cathedral of Learning at the University of Pittsburgh, the library could not escape its context as a building caught between the desire to preserve religion within academic life and secular concerns shaping the modern university. That the library's iconography could be read on a spectrum from sincere ecclesiastical emulation to a parody of a religious past points exactly to this transformative moment for religion on the campus in the early twentieth century. William Harlan Hale's attack on Yale's "cathedral orgy" for failing to meet modern conditions describes just how fragile religion's position in the university now was.

CHAPTER 5

THE POSTWAR CHAPEL AT MIT

In 1956, the National Council of Churches named the chapels at the Massachusetts Institute of Technology and the Illinois Institute of Technology among the eighteen best examples of modern church architecture in the United States since 1930.[1] The MIT Chapel (1950–55) by Eero Saarinen and the Robert F. Carr Memorial Chapel of St. Saviour (1949–52) by Ludwig Mies van der Rohe at IIT were a great departure from the monumental campus chapels of the early twentieth century (figs. 5.1, 5.2). The MIT Chapel, while positioned conventionally within the new campus center, appeals to a primitive image of a sacred space in order to accommodate Protestant, Catholic, and Jewish worship. The IIT chapel bears no external indication of its religious identity—no steeple, no cross, no towering height—and occupies an inconspicuous place on campus. Their small size—each chapel seats about one hundred worshippers—further evinced the shift from communal worship typically dominated by a Protestant or broad Christian tradition to individual worship respectful of different faiths. The strikingly modern forms of the MIT and IIT chapels, respectively christened the "gas tank" and the "God box," challenged conventional chapel design and presented a new image of religion in the modern university.[2]

Figure 5.1. Massachusetts Institute of Technology Chapel, Eero Saarinen with Bruce Adams, 1950–55, Massachusetts Institute of Technology, Cambridge, photograph ca. 1955. Courtesy MIT Museum.

Figure 5.2. Eastern entrance facade of the Robert F. Carr Memorial Chapel of St. Saviour, Ludwig Mies van der Rohe, 1949–52, Illinois Institute of Technology, Chicago. IIT Archives, Paul V. Galvin Library, Illinois Institute of Technology, Chicago.

Yet despite their differences from the large neo-Gothic and neo-Colonial chapels at Princeton and Harvard, those at MIT and IIT possessed the same intention: Their presence asserted the importance of moral character and knowledge revealed through religious faith. Even for these technological schools whose reputations rested primarily on their scientific, engineering, and architectural prowess, science alone did not possess the whole truth. Religion and the humanities revealed a vital truth of their own, leading to codes of ethics and morality essential to human life. World War II had underscored the need for scientists to demonstrate a social responsibility and to consider the implications of their inventions and discoveries. The MIT administration reexamined its educational mission in the postwar era, concluding that the university had "a right and a responsibility to deal with ideals as well as ideas and to be concerned with the search for virtue while we become proficient in the search for things."[3] IIT envisioned its mission as both fostering "the fundamental research that is the bedrock of all industry" and producing "socially conscious graduates who will be assets to their communities as well as to their professions."[4] The chapels on their campuses symbolized the scientist's responsibility in the moral, ethical use of scientific knowledge in the world.

The construction of chapels at MIT and IIT also exemplified the postwar religious revival in the United States. In the late 1940s, an overwhelming number of Americans identified with a religious denomination even if they did not attend services, and church building reached new highs.[5] From $26 million in 1945, church construction costs rose to $409 million in 1950 and to $935 million in 1959, before declining in the 1960s.[6] Such religious enthusiasm extended to the college and university campus, leading Merrimon Cuninggim in *The College Seeks Religion* to claim in 1947 that "religion occupies a larger place in the colleges' thinking and practice than at any time in the twentieth century."[7] The physical campus affirmed this revival. The 1950s in particular saw a construction boom in religious buildings on the American campus, in what would be the last major boom of the twentieth century. During this period, the Danforth Chapel program, funded by the philanthropist William H. Danforth, spurred the construction of small, meditative worship spaces on more than fifteen public university and college campuses.[8]

Yet these Danforth Chapels, like those at MIT and IIT, were small scaled and humble in architectural form, responding to a new need to respect religious diversity. The three separate Protestant, Catholic, and Jewish worship spaces at Brandeis University, a notably Jewish institution, by the architects Harrison and Abramovitz, completed in 1955, also showed a path for accommodating religious difference. Religion was indeed on campus (even the public campus), but it was dramatically changed in visual expression. The campus chapel could no longer possess an overtly Christian image. So too did the scale need to be smaller and in many cases the location less central. The postwar campus chapel needed to visualize the changed role of religion in the university.

Among the various postwar chapels on the American campus, the MIT Chapel especially represents a sophisticated narrative of a preeminent technological school's response to world events and its administration's desire to include the moral and social education of its scientists. Eero Saarinen's modern interpretation of the New England meetinghouse and common for the MIT campus embodied the university's new commitment to social and moral awareness in the wake of World War II. Revealed knowledge still had an important role to play even in an institution where empirical knowledge reigned supreme. Yet the rhetoric in support of religion at midcentury proved far more powerful than the chapel form itself. No longer monumental or overtly Christian, the MIT Chapel, like other postwar chapels, used minimalist imagery to accommodate more inclusive worship on a reduced scale. Religion was on campus but transformed, its visual authority diminished.

IMAGINING A CHAPEL FOR MIT

For MIT's new campus in Cambridge, the architect and MIT alumnus William Welles Bosworth constructed a version of the Great White City on the horizon of the Charles River in the early twentieth century.[9] This Technology-on-the-Charles overlaid the image of a cultural center on a site of scientific production to elevate the status of MIT. The white hue of the Indiana limestone, Ionic pilasters and columns, and inscribed names of great scientists, engineers, and philosophers like Charles Darwin and Aristotle on the building's attic suggested classical learning instead of factory production. The courtyards carved within the U-shape composition of the principal building were to create "an atmosphere of academic life" and to "counterbalance to some degree the sterner phases which are so strongly impressed upon the student in the field of applied science, especially in this institution."[10] No chapel building, however, was included in this original development of MIT's campus to address students' religious life. Students either attended services in local churches or those held in classrooms, and the Technology Christian Association occupied office space in the student union. Some

accounts suggested that the reason MIT did not have a chapel was so
that the institution would not compete with surrounding churches. Indeed, the integration of students in Cambridge and Boston churches
helped to bridge the divide between town and gown. Yet from the view
from Boston, religion did not appear to count prominently in the education of the scientist.

In 1938, on the verge of World War II, Bosworth, now approaching
his seventies, was given the opportunity to design a chapel for MIT.[11]
That year had put a special emphasis on moral questions, a point that
Bosworth himself made: "Certainly this is a most propitious moment in
the history of the world, when the contrasts of Christ and Anti-Christ
are so evident in international ethics today, for the chapel question to be
agitated."[12] The meeting of Germany's Adolf Hitler with Prime Minister Neville Chamberlain of Great Britain, Premier Édouard Daladier of
France, and Benito Mussolini of Italy in Munich two months earlier had
produced a redrawn map of Europe, giving Hitler control of Austria.
Time would later name Hitler its "Person of the Year" for 1938 in recognition of the terrifying and powerful role that Germany had assumed
in European affairs.

Bosworth envisioned the chapel in the continuum of his original
designs for MIT, but it was also a chapel that took to heart its standing within a scientific institute. On a site fronting the river, Bosworth
proposed a white, classical, domed, Greek cross chapel (fig. 5.3). Essential to the chapel's design was the campanile, whose chimes were to
"serve also as a sort of reminder of the chapel and what it stands for
to the reflecting mind, throughout the hours of the day and night."[13]
At night, the campanile's light would be a "sort of electric torch, with
a searchlight in its top, searching the heavens, as it were, for Truth,
thus symbolizing the purposes for which the institution stands."[14] In
Bosworth's interpretation, truth resided in both religious worship and
scientific investigation. The examination of truth in the chapel and the
examination of truth in the laboratory were to be united in this one
building.

In exterior and interior treatment, Bosworth designed a chapel
classical in form, a play on the Roman Pantheon. He dictated that the

Figure 5.3. Perspective drawing of proposed chapel for MIT showing the southern entrance facade facing the Charles River, William Welles Bosworth, 1938. Massachusetts Institute of Technology, Office of the President, records of Karl Taylor Compton and James Rhyne Killian, AC 4, box 33, Massachusetts Institute of Technology, Institute Archives and Special Collections, Cambridge.

exterior "should be exceedingly plain," with the exception of low-relief sculptures of the prophets or angels such as Michael and Gabriel flanking the upper windows. The interior plan included the familiar arrangement of auditorium seating, pulpit, and altar. Soft, indirect lighting and a palate of green, gold, and brown in reference to nature would foster a meditative atmosphere. Drawing the eye upward, the circular opening of the dome was to include "in mosaic a ring of angels in white and gold, adapted from Blake's morning starts singing together; and in the center, on white clouds, the dove, emblematic of the Spirit 'ascending and descending upon the Son of Man, in whom I am well pleased.'" For the exterior, Bosworth suggested that the inscription on the frieze over the main portico read "dedicated to the unfolding spiritual life of man." This inscription, "which will always carry the message of the importance of the 'imponderables' in the development of man," was to emphasize the place of religion in MIT's mission.[15]

If the chapel was classic in form, its centerpiece was fantastic. On the altar, "instead of candles and cross or tabernacle, which would offend the 'free thinker,'" Bosworth proposed "a great vertical glass panel illuminated by some throbbing, pulsating, electrical currents, which no one knows better how to produce than the experts at Technology, and which would express . . . the presence and the activity of the creative energy and life that has made us and of which we are a part."[16] This electrified glass panel would fuse the institute's scientific interests with the recognition of a higher force. Bosworth's chapel proposal and its fantastic altar were the beginnings of an explicit visual and architectural statement of the importance of religion even in an institution devoted to science. While it was not to be constructed, William Welles Bosworth's 1938 chapel design nevertheless foreshadowed the concerns about world events and MIT's refocused educational mission that shaped the chapel's ultimate form.

EDUCATING THE MORAL SCIENTIST

If the specter of Nazi Germany prompted Bosworth's chapel proposal shortly before World War II, the powerful display of technology at war's end intensified the relationship between science and morality and made acute the absence of a chapel at MIT. The dropping of the atomic bomb on Hiroshima and Nagasaki brought into sharp focus the power that schools like MIT produced. The Institute had in fact played a large role in technological development for the war. Roughly $117 million in government contracts to the school funded research into chemical engineering, oxygen production, and the development of radar. Military forces came to MIT to train in the use of the radar detection system. MIT president Carl T. Compton was a member of the committee that advised President Harry Truman on the decision to use the atomic bomb.[17] The war's end triggered a period of introspection at MIT and a review of its academic mission.

The MIT administration, first under Compton (1930–48) and subsequently under James R. Killian (1948–59), spent the postwar years examining the need to put science in a broader social context. In 1947, MIT's Committee on Educational Survey issued the Lewis Report, which reinforced the need to bolster humanities study.[18] As President Killian summarized it, "We need better linkages between science and the humanities, with the object of fusing the two into a broad humanism that rests upon both science and the liberal arts and that does not weaken either. We need bifocal vision to thread our way among the problems of modern society."[19]

At the committee's recommendation, MIT in the late 1940s established the School of Humanities and Social Studies, which grew to include studies in literature, music, theater, the visual arts, archaeology, linguistics, psychology, and philosophy and attracted such notable scholars as the linguist Noam Chomsky. By 1955, MIT offered not only its Course XIV, a broad course in the social sciences, but also Course XXI, which alternated on themes of the American Industrial Society and Philosophy and Literature and allowed students to choose a double major in the humanities or social science and engineering or science.[20] The broadening of MIT's curriculum suggested that concerns other than science also deserved close inspection and were to play a part in the education of its scientists.

The most public examination of MIT's conscience came at the 1949 Mid-Century Convocation on the Social Implications of Scientific Progress.[21] Dominating the event was the speech by former British prime minister, Sir Winston Churchill. One Harvard student's pointed question, "How did you persuade Winston to speak to those steam fitters of yours?," to the organizer of the convocation bitingly underscored the Institute's public status as a technical—and only technical—school and its need to find ways to visibly proclaim its commitment to a larger understanding of the place of science in the world.[22]

Though Churchill's speech is perhaps most remembered for its Cold War references, it carried an insistent message that science must be subservient to moral and religious concerns. Speaking at the Boston Garden arena against the backdrop of an aerial view of Bosworth's classical buildings, Churchill minced no words in setting forth proper priorities, even for a dominantly technological school:

> No technical knowledge can outweigh knowledge of the humanities in the gaining of which philosophy and history walk hand in hand. Our inheritance of well-founded slowly conceived codes of honour, morals and manners, the passionate convictions which so many hundreds of millions share together of the principles of freedom and justice, are far more precious to us than anything which scientific discoveries could bestow. Those whose minds are attracted or compelled to rigid and symmetrical systems of government should remember that logic, like science, must be the servant and not the master of man.[23]

Killian and his administration firmly believed that a chapel building was essential to fostering this moral and social awareness. In 1950, one year after the convocation, the administration submitted a grant proposal to the Kresge Foundation, including a request for funding for an auditorium and chapel. The grant application acknowledged "that the scientist has failed to take his appropriate share of responsibility for solving the social problems which have evolved in the wake of his successes." In addition to constructing a chapel, the MIT administration wanted to institute a "program of education and indoctrination in the responsibilities of citizenship and in those qualities of character and ideals which are basic to a good society, and to which the principles of Christ give, in turn, the individual basis."[24]

This desire to inculcate religion and morality in education—to not only train scientists but moral citizens as well—perpetuated the Oxbridge ideal of developing the whole student. Killian made explicit MIT's commitment to the spiritual and ethical life of its students in his 1954 statement on the Institute's religious program. He asserted that MIT must "give attention to man's spiritual life" and "encourage an

understanding of those postulates which underlie our society's concept of virtue." Put plainly, "The responsibility to deal with these great
matters is inherent in any program to educate young people adequately
and broadly. Their all-round development requires a growth of the
spirit as well as the mind."[25] Killian viewed the development of students' spiritual life as of a piece with MIT's humanities program. This
combination of scientific, humanistic, and spiritual programs defined
MIT's postwar mission.

This statement on religious life at MIT also made bold claims about
science's contribution to religion. Reversing the typical contention that
religion offered larger, fundamental context for science's discoveries,
President Killian argued that science itself had much to offer religion.
"An institute of science," he wrote, "may well be an environment especially favorable to deeper spiritual insights."[26] In his explanation, Killian made a remarkable statement cementing his belief in the unity of
the good, the beautiful, and the true, a statement that recalled Columbia University president Nicholas Murray Butler's defense of the Foucault pendulum experiment in St. Paul's Chapel nearly half a century
earlier. Science, Killian believed, emphasized "the importance of truth
and of the value of brotherhood and its revelation of the beauty, the
order, the majesty, the wonder of man and of the universe around him."
And those attentive to both science and religion could "advance man's
search for virtue and understanding with new vigor and in new ways."[27]
As the new dean of students, William Speer, whom Killian had asked to
review his statement on religion, clarified, scientific investigation offered
new insights into religion because "man can avail himself in a way that
he has not been able to previously of the revelation of himself which
God makes in the physical universe, and so gain from man's end a dimension which God always had put there but which only science has
opened up from the human end."[28] This liberal Protestant belief that
science and religion sought the same ends echoed the arguments made
in the early twentieth century for the cooperation between science and
religion.

MIT in the mid-twentieth century thus believed that religion and
science were partners in the search for truth. Especially in the modern
age, MIT had a responsibility to foster the moral and ethical awareness

of its student scientists. The MIT administration wished to communicate scientists' need for a moral and social consciousness, and they looked toward an architectural expression of religion to do so.

A MEETING HOUSE ON THE COMMON FOR MIT

The conception of a twentieth-century meetinghouse for MIT came from Dean of Students Everett Moore Baker. A graduate of the Harvard Divinity School and a Unitarian minister, Baker had long listened to complaints from the Technology Christian Association and the Catholic association of students that there was no worship space on campus.[29] The desire to "relieve the driving atmosphere characteristic of MIT" and the belief that "there ought to be something other than books and labs" further made the case for a dedicated worship space.[30] In December 1949, just before the grant proposal to the Kresge Foundation, Baker submitted a proposal for a chapel space to President Killian. Much like the arguments for a new chapel at Yale University in the 1920s, Baker asserted that a chapel building was equally important to the library and the laboratories in communicating the mission of the Institute:

> MIT's laboratories and lecture halls, and now its Library, stand as great symbols of man's search for truth in the realm of the material, the physical and the cultural—the lack of a chapel and the facilities it would afford to the enrichment of the spiritual in the life of our students and Faculty is immediately evident within and without the community.[31]

To make his case, Baker appealed to the historical role of the meetinghouse and church in New England and in Massachusetts in particular: "It is difficult to think of America without the village church and the meeting house. It is equally difficult to imagine MIT of tomorrow fulfilling its many responsibilities to our nation and our world without its chapel and its meeting house."[32]

President Killian, also a practicing Unitarian, agreed. He seized on Baker's meetinghouse imagery as shorthand to describe MIT's new emphasis on social and moral responsibility both within the institute and in the larger world. The meetinghouse conveyed the sense that religion, or at least morality, formed the foundation for social responsibility. In colonial and early America, as the religious historian Peter Williams has explained, the meetinghouse was the space where civil and divine law commingled and reinforced each other. It represented a harmony between religious and civic life.[33] A meetinghouse at MIT would evince the belief in socially responsible science and the expanded humanities program.

Killian and others in his administration were careful, however, to separate the meetinghouse concept from its Protestant heritage. MIT was a private institution with a staunch nonsectarian policy, and World War II had put a special emphasis on the need for sensitivity to Protestant, Catholic, and Jewish equality. This was affirmed in the 1954 statement on MIT's religious life, which called for "an atmosphere of religious freedom."[34] As much as Killian and his administration wished to emphasize the religious and the spiritual life at MIT, they encountered a postwar landscape in which historical Protestant hegemony had to be mitigated.

Given this nonsectarian emphasis, the new meetinghouse at MIT could not imitate its Protestant forerunners in form. A blueprint plan accompanying Dean Baker's written chapel proposal sketched a dramatically different religious space. Instead of one unified space, Baker suggested two: a larger 1,000- to 1,200-seat auditorium and a smaller devotional chapel seating about 75. A small chapel would not "compete with community churches and would be suitable for all users," and since MIT did not have a compulsory chapel requirement monumental worship space was unnecessary.[35] The auditorium was to accommodate larger worship services as well as secular concerts and theater productions. Although this multipurpose auditorium made practical sense and although Dean Baker, a minister, had a vested interest in promoting religion, his proposed separation of the auditorium and the dedicated chapel would ultimately assign a secondary status to the chapel vis-à-vis the auditorium in the MIT landscape.

Dean Baker's meetinghouse proposal was the foundation for the new religious buildings at the Massachusetts Institute of Technology.

Using the proposal as a guideline, MIT's grant request to the Kresge Foundation included a provision "for a small, but dignified chapel" and associated auditorium.[36] The Kresge Foundation awarded MIT a $1.5 million grant to fund the buildings' construction in 1950.

EERO SAARINEN'S CYLINDER AND DOME

The choice of the noted modernist Eero Saarinen as the architect of the chapel and meetinghouse signaled a commitment by MIT to progressive modern architecture. While the university generally chose architects from the Boston area for its campus commissions, its building committee asserted that the project, given its particular program, required "the best architect, regardless of his location."[37] The decision to give Saarinen the commission, President James Killian said, "reflects our conviction here at MIT that an institution devoted to advancing the boundaries of knowledge should also be creative and pioneering in its own architecture."[38]

Saarinen transformed the idea of a chapel and meetinghouse into a new campus center at MIT's western edge (fig. 5.4). In his plan for this center, not fully realized, the domed auditorium bordered the western edge near the playing fields; the cylindrical chapel was positioned near Massachusetts Avenue, where several existing buildings, including the residential, Tudor-style Bexley Hall, were to be demolished; and an eight-story student center defined the northern boundary. A low, linear strip including administration offices was to connect the chapel and the auditorium, offered a covered walkway, and defined the plaza's southern border. Trees and landscaping further shaped the plaza's edges and sheltered the meditative chapel.[39] With the proposed depression of Massachusetts Avenue fifteen feet below grade, a broad bridge would link William Welles Bosworth's original MIT buildings to Saarinen's expansive plaza raised three feet above street level.[40]

The plaza and its attendant auditorium, chapel, and future student union building were to provide the "focus in a college community that has no real center to date," in the words of the *Architectural Forum*.[41] MIT's long-term campus planning goals segregated the academic buildings to

Figure 5.4. Eero Saarinen's plan for the MIT plaza overlaid on a photograph of the existing MIT campus, ca. 1952. The plaza includes the domed auditorium, the cylindrical chapel, and the future rectilinear student union building. From "Saarinen Challenges the Rectangle," *Architectural Forum* 98, no. 1 (January 1953): 132.

the east of Massachusetts Avenue and housing and extracurricular life to the west.[42] The proposed plaza's proximity to MIT's new residential buildings, including Alvar Aalto's Baker House (1946–48), strengthened the association of the meetinghouse with the extracurricular life of MIT while capitalizing on the proximity to Massachusetts Avenue. Moreover, Saarinen's plaza created an internal center that supported "the fact that we are tending to turn inward toward the west campus with the general thought that life at the Institute will be centered back away from the street."[43] This inward plaza fulfilled the same function as the Oxbridge quadrangle in promoting a close-knit community of scholars. The new campus common was to embody the corporate life of MIT.

For Kresge Auditorium, Saarinen with partner Bruce Adams imagined a form that stood in stark contrast to MIT's original early-twentieth-century buildings by William Welles Bosworth (fig. 5.5). To design the auditorium as a "box-like structure" mimicking the surrounding buildings would have been "an undistinguished anticlimax to the space" in Saarinen's view. He instead designed a dome for the 1,200-seat Kresge Auditorium as a "contrasting silhouette."[44] The auditorium simultaneously departs from Bosworth's classical design and emulates it. The dome provides a sharp contrast to the horizontal and vertical lines of the original buildings while echoing its domes. The lightness of the dome also plays off the heaviness of Bosworth's buildings. In actuality one-eighth of a sphere shaped like a trefoil and connected to the ground at three points, the dome stands independent of the glass and steel that infills its arches. "A dome of thin-shell concrete," Saarinen reasoned, "seemed right for a university interested in progressive architecture."[45]

The chapel itself is a foil to the auditorium (see fig. 5.5). Whereas the domed auditorium is sail-like, balanced on three points, and transparent, the cylindrical chapel is monumental, grounded, and windowless. The auditorium and the chapel are opposites in both materials and scale. The solid red brick of the chapel, chosen to match the material of the surrounding dormitories, contrasts with the white concrete and clear glazing of the auditorium.[46] With about 120 seats, the chapel accommodates only about one-tenth the number of the auditorium, though it can appear to rival the scale of the auditorium depending on

Figure 5.5. View of the MIT Chapel (left) and the Kresge Auditorium (right). Courtesy MIT Museum.

one's vantage point in the plaza. Whereas the windows of the auditorium reflect the gaze back on the plaza's whole composition, keeping in sight the chapel and MIT's original buildings, the chapel's lack of windows stresses its meditative environment and protects it from the noise and bustle of Massachusetts Avenue.

Creating this meditative environment was a principal concern in the design of the chapel. Killian expressed the wish that the chapel "in its plan and in its relationship to courts and other external features should capture a sense of repose and quiet. We need at the Institute more places where one can escape from the madding crowd and find peace and solitude."[47] Saarinen designed an entrance sequence that creates a sense of separation and transition from the rest of the MIT campus. A brick wall screens the chapel from Massachusetts Avenue and the neighboring dormitory, Bexley Hall, which was not torn down according to Saarinen's original plan. Students and visitors reach the chapel's entrance past trees and other landscaping up a ramp to the entrance vestibule, which includes an elevator and a stair leading to the auxiliary rooms below. The narthex, lined with translucent glass, links the entrance vestibule to the sanctuary. It is also a bridge crossing over the water-filled moat encircling the sanctuary cylinder. Walking through this narthex provides the physical transition between the outside world and the chapel space. The narthex serves, in the words of Saarinen, "as a sort of decompression chamber."[48]

The blank exterior of the cylindrical sanctuary belies the majesty of its interior (fig. 5.6). As the chapel was to be used by numerous faiths, Saarinen and Adams could not employ any specific religious iconography. Instead, they turned toward the powerful effects of light to appeal to "basic spiritual feelings."[49] On the exterior, irregularly sized arches at the base of the brick cylinder allow light into the chapel's interior, where an independent secondary wall of a serpentine, undulating shape actually forms the interior (fig. 5.7). The light drawn through the glass between the exterior and interior walls reflects off the water in the chapel's moat, creating a grotto effect of soft, dappled light ringing the perimeter of the building. Above the solid marble pedestal raised upon a dais of three concentric circles, a skylight emits a focused halo of light. The "soft, mysterious secondary light" is a "foil" to this direct light, Saarinen explained. Together, these lights conveyed an "atmosphere of spiritual unworldliness."[50]

A golden metal sculpture by Harry Bertoia, composed of small rectangular metal pieces strung to make a screen, captures and reflects the light from above and from below. Though not the electrified version that Bosworth had proposed for the altar in his chapel design, this abstract sculpture similarly provides a meditative focal point. Individual chairs instead of pews fill the floor space of the chapel, and an organ resides in a loft at the back. Otherwise, the interior of the chapel is plain, its walls decorated only by the irregular brickwork to further add to a sense of texture to the interior.[51] "I am happy with the interior of the chapel," Saarinen said. "I think we managed to make it a place where an individual can contemplate things larger than himself."[52]

Figure 5.6. Interior of the MIT Chapel. Courtesy MIT Museum.

Figure 5.7. Interior of the MIT Chapel showing the undulating walls with light coming from the moat. Courtesy MIT Museum.

The appeal to light and primitive and abstract forms sought to sensitively resolve the chapel's extraordinarily difficult multidenominational worship program in the context of a technological school. From the historian Martin Marty's perspective, the MIT chapel had met its charge admirably:

> There [at MIT], Eero Saarinen has come near the point of perfection in meeting a situation of great complexity. The building must imply that religion has something to say to a technical age and to one of that age's symbolic centers. One chapel must serve all faiths. For that reason the architect could not rely on conventional and specific religious symbols. He had simply to provide "holy emptiness" that many men can worship there. The screen devised by Harry Bertoia capturing brightness from the "dome of light" above has helped furnish this arena for confrontation of man and God. Simple, stark brick walls within a circular form (the cave for withdrawal) propose the kind of primitiveness, the new beginning we have been seeking.[53]

The primitive "cave for withdrawal" did have religious allusions. Saarinen and Adams had considered other shapes for the chapel, including a rectangle and a smaller dome to echo that of the auditorium. However, in choosing the cylindrical shape—the source of the "gas tank" nickname—the architects were alluding to Judeo-Christian symbolism.[54] The cylinder recalled the circular shapes of baptisteries; the cylinder's immersion into a water-filled moat, the act of baptism.[55] The abstract aluminum bell tower and spire on top of the chapel also is a conventionally Christian device. In his explanation of the tower and spire, however, the sculptor Theodore Roszak said that the forms possessed multidenominational meanings. While the vertical forms of bell tower and spire were "basically 'gothic'" and evoked "a simplified version of the gargoyle" of Christian iconography, the three vertical lines of the sculpture consciously represented the three traditions—Protestant, Catholic, and Jewish—that shared the worship space, and they together related to "the symbol of the trinity as well as the recurrent forms of the 2 superimposed triangles in the 'Star of David.'"[56] The chapel therefore appealed to religious symbolism, but it did so in a sensitive way that allowed Christians as well as Jews to worship comfortably within its walls.

Saarinen's MIT Chapel remains an icon of modernist design, often discussed in architectural surveys for its sublime and sacred interior. But when examined in the context of MIT's campus and educational mission, the chapel's success is not as brilliant. This was acknowledged early on, even by Saarinen himself. The chapel and the auditorium failed to create a unifying center for MIT. Five years after the chapel and auditorium dedication, Saarinen himself judged the dome and the cylinder as "too egocentric." In his design, Saarinen had "conceived of these buildings as buildings on a great square" and hoped to create "one homogeneous whole—in a sense continue the spirit of the Bosworth buildings—not in actual architecture but in largeness of spirit." However, the forms themselves "are closed and they do not contribute anything to creating a unity within an area which so sadly needs unity."[57]

Neither do the buildings assert a strong message about religion on MIT's campus. Despite the inscription in its lobby, "The Kresge Auditorium—The Meeting House of the Massachusetts Institute of Technology," the auditorium conveys little affiliation with a religious purpose. Its futuristic dome shape and glass and metal materiality hint at nothing of religious symbolism. At best, it is a secular meetinghouse. While the chapel's interior is a critical success, the chapel as a whole makes only a token gesture to religious imagery. In the context of the larger campus, the architectural image of the MIT Chapel is diminished. Its small size and abstracted form speak to a private, meditative, and small-scale religious experience vastly different from the overt, communal, and Christian-dominated image of religion on campus in the interwar decades.

RHETORIC AND REALITY AT MIT

If the chapel was indeed a weakened religious form, the enthusiastic dedicatory speeches given in May 1955 offered no hint of it. The strident rhetoric, in full agreement with MIT's decision to renew a focus on religion, returned to Winston Churchill's earlier claim that science could not reign supreme in the world. Keynote speaker Eelco N. van Kleffens—a former ambassador to the United States, a former president of the United Nations General Assembly, and then the Netherlands ambassador to Portugal—emphasized this rebalancing of religion and science in modern life. The limits of technology, he claimed, had become clear. Van Kleffens warned of "a danger inherent in technological education and research" that "may lead to an undue narrowing of belief and faith," "may make man forgetful of divine and human laws," and may induce a state of mind "in which no place is left for belief except in what we see demonstrated in the test tube."[58] This sense that science did not hold all the answers was echoed by the Reverend Theodore P. Ferris, rector of Boston's Trinity Church, who represented the MIT Corporation in the affirmation address. Ferris looked upon the new MIT buildings with a sense of optimism. From his perspective, they were "a sign of a change in climate," a retreat from the presumption "that there was nothing beyond the reach of our inquiring minds."[59]

What science desperately needed was the addition of a religious and moral perspective. The increase in science's power only heightened this need. "The more scientific training [the student] has, the more he needs the complementary cultivation of his heart and spirit," Reverend Ferris contended. "The more power science miraculously places in his hands, the more he needs a sense of moral values to guide him in the use of that power."[60] Religion provided something that science could not give itself: the rules governing how to use science's fruits. Van Kleffens pointedly stated, "Man may not do with his knowledge as he pleases. There may be no boundary to what he may discover, but there *is* a boundary to what he may do with the discovery."[61] Religion and the humanities together described that boundary, and they therefore remained a crucial part of higher education. But the admission of religion's importance in a technical institution did not discount science's contributions. Ferris affirmed that religion and science "go together hand in hand. Religion without science is almost sure to become superstition, and science without religion is almost as sure to become a lifeless skeleton of facts and figures."[62]

Like every other college and university chapel, the MIT Chapel was to be the visual symbol of the needed religious perspective in higher education. In an admonishment to MIT, van Kleffens warned, "Let the new chapel, and also the auditorium, remain a constant warning that, just as technology cannot exhaust truth, it is not qualified, and therefore should not attempt, to monopolize belief."[63] But this rhetoric was far stronger than the message the chapel itself asserted. Even as MIT's leadership continued in the belief that higher education needed to attend to religious, moral, and spiritual concerns, religion on campus by the mid-twentieth century could no longer be imposed on students, practiced on a large scale, or attuned to only one religious perspective. If religion was to be practiced on the nondenominational campus, it needed to be voluntary, respectful of varying faith traditions, and small scale. The now necessarily small chapel could no longer be a forceful advertisement for religion, and its often peripheral location spoke to religion's removal from the main mission of the university. Eero Saarinen's MIT Chapel was beautiful, but ultimately it was a beautiful white elephant, despite its endorsers' optimistic hopes to the contrary.

EPILOGUE

College and university chapels underwent profound changes in their architectural form in the forty years from the 1920s to the 1960s as religion on campus was caught in the sea change of modernity. The rise of science, the German research model of higher education, and the end of a centuries-long tradition of compulsory chapel signaled an era of secularization. While university leaders recognized this shift, they maintained the goal of educating the whole student, including his spiritual life, and sought ways to preserve religion on campus. Architecture became a way to argue for religion's continued relevance. Large-scale chapels acted as advertisements of religion, lavish neo-Gothic interiors appealed to students' emotions, and chapels at the campus center suggested religion's lasting significance to the university mission. There also arose new kinds of cathedrals on campus, like the University of Pittsburgh's Cathedral of Learning and Yale's Sterling Memorial Library, whose religious metaphors crafted a pervasive religious backdrop for scientific work. In the immediate postwar years, chapel building was still prevalent, but these much smaller, nondenominational worship spaces spoke to a changed religious landscape. As much as leaders sought to keep religion relevant to the modern American university, the diminishing image of religious architecture on campus revealed that religion shared, and eventually ceded, its once-preeminent role on the American campus.

The image of university religion on the private, nondenominational university campus remains that crafted in these interwar and immediate postwar years. From the 1960s forward, the impulse to build religious structures on the nondenominational campus was greatly weakened. The lack of compulsory and community-wide worship rendered new religious buildings unnecessary, and the drive to accommodate a range of beliefs—now expanded beyond the Judeo-Christian core to include Islam, Hinduism, and Buddhism, among others—as well as nonbelief made constructing a worship space problematic to meet all constituencies. While college and university chapels are still used for worship services, memorials, funerals, weddings, and commencements, religion is no longer central to the vast majority of nondenominational universities, and so these worship spaces are marginalized. These chapels have become white elephants in the context of the university mission.

This is not to proclaim the end of religious building on the American campus wholesale. In the 1950s and 1960s, denominational campuses in the United States witnessed another building boom that included religious spaces. Outstanding examples from this era are Eero Saarinen's chapel for Concordia Lutheran Theological Seminary (1953–58), the Chapel of the Resurrection (1959) at Valparaiso University, also Lutheran, and the fantastic futuristic campus of Oral Roberts University, a Charismatic Christian institution, featuring the Prayer Tower from the 1960s. Paul Rudolph designed the interdenominational Tuskegee University Chapel (1960–69) and later the William R. Cannon Chapel (1979–81) at Emory University, historically affiliated with the Methodist Church. These chapels followed the architectural currents of their time, including late modernism and brutalism, and were often large in size to accommodate a university community still united in a common mode of worship. Chapel building continues today, again on denominational campuses. Philip Johnson designed the postmodern St. Basil Chapel (2007) for the Catholic campus of St. Thomas University in Houston, Texas. A 1,100-seat Catholic chapel was constructed for Ave Maria University, opened in 2007, in Florida.

The practice of religion, too, is far from absent on campus. At Harvard, the church holds regular morning prayer, in addition to a Sunday Protestant service. The Princeton University Chapel hosts an interdenominational Protestant service, a Catholic mass, and an Episcopal service each Sunday. A Catholic Blessed Sacrament chapel was recently instituted in one part of the Princeton chapel for Eucharistic adoration, and Catholic masses are held daily. At the MIT Chapel, Catholic, interdenominational Protestant, Lutheran, and Buddhist services are offered each week, and Jewish and Muslim services now take place at the MIT Religious Activities Center nearby. Off campus, even more services are held in buildings that ring the university. Catholic Newman Centers, Methodist Wesleyan Centers, Jewish Hillels, and others cater to denominational interests at private and public universities. They house a vibrant sectarian religious life, allowing for participation in any number of faith traditions without the concern of a careful, legal nondenominational identity.

But for private nondenominational campuses, such as Harvard, Yale, and Princeton, the era of important chapel building is over. Religion's role has been relegated to the periphery and removed from the essential education of its students, as the failure of Harvard University in 2006 to include a required course under the rubric "Reason and Faith" in its core curriculum illustrates.[1] The central mission of the university has been defined in other terms. Although religious services continue in these historic chapels, they are in numbers typically in the low hundreds rather than the thousands. While secularism cannot be said to be complete, the postmodern emphasis on accommodation of all religions and nonbelief complicates the visual expression of religion on the campus. The religious architecture on campus that was constructed in the early twentieth century—the last era of widespread chapel building on the campus—is a vestige of a Protestant hegemony that even then was being challenged.

The uncertainty over religion's role in the university, and what to do with religious buildings and symbols, continues today. In 2006, the College of William & Mary, originally founded as an Anglican institution in 1693 and transformed into a public college in 1906, found itself confronting the clash of a religious legacy with modern circumstances.

What began as a controversy focused on a cross was in the end a re-vealing discussion of the meaning and role of a historic chapel in a changed institution.

William & Mary's historic Wren Building included a chapel com-pleted in 1732. During renovations of the chapel in the 1930s (part of the larger remaking of Colonial Williamsburg funded by John D. Rocke-feller Jr.), nearby Burton Parish loaned an eighteen-inch brass cross for display in the William & Mary chapel (fig. 6.1). In the context of 1930s America, where the Protestant hold on higher education was still preva-lent if declining, the display of a cross went unquestioned. But by 2006, complaints about the cross being displayed in the chapel space — a space regularly used for nonreligious events — reached William & Mary president Gene R. Nichol Jr. Without first consulting the William & Mary community, Nichol decided to remove the cross from permanent display on the altar. The cross would, however, be available for display on request.

The decision quickly met a cacophony of protest. Initially, the con-troversy was internal to the college community and centered on Nichol's unilateral decision to remove the cross. But the controversy quickly be-came a national media topic and a cause célèbre for the political right. Those in support of the cross, including such conservatives as Newt Gingrich, pointed to its removal as a sign of increased secularization in the United States and a case of political correctness gone too far. To this group, Nichol's move promoted the preference of the few against the desire of the many, denied the College's historic identity, and alien-ated Christians in the name of welcoming people of all faiths.

To President Nichol, the removal of the cross was a necessary ac-tion to erase any suggestion of exclusion in this public college. In his explanation of his actions, Nichol, himself a Catholic and a former professor of constitutional law, wrote, "Though we haven't meant to do so, the display of a Christian cross — the most potent symbol of my own religion — in the heart of our most important building sends an unmistakable message that the chapel belongs more fully to some of us than others."[2] But the outrage over the cross removal forced Nichol to moderate his decision. Just months after the initial announcement, Nichol instituted a new policy to display the cross all day on Sundays

Figure 6.1. Interior of the Wren Chapel at the College of William & Mary, showing the cross displayed above the table. Photograph by Margaret M. Grubiak.

and planned a plaque for the chapel to "commemorate the Chapel's origins as an Anglican place of worship and symbol of the Christian beginnings of the College."[3] In announcing the amended policy, Nichol asserted firmly, "But what I am not willing to do is compromise on that fundamental principle of equal access for all."[4]

Yet the issue was far from settled. Less than four months after the cross's removal from permanent display, a crush of students, alumni, and community members gathered in the Wren Chapel to listen to a formal debate titled, "Religion in the Campus: Should the Cross be Reinstated in the Wren Chapel?" The debate's major sponsor was the Intercollegiate Studies Institute (ISI), a nonprofit, conservative-leaning organization.[5] Conservative commentator Dinesh D'Souza, who held liberals responsible in part for the 9/11 attacks and whose book, *What's So Great about Christianity*, would be published just six months after the debate, argued the affirmative position.[6] President Nichol had been invited to be D'Souza's opponent, but Nichol reportedly avoided the invitation. Arguing the negative position instead was William & Mary professor of religious studies, David L. Holmes.[7] The cross in question stood as the backdrop of the debate.

While D'Souza and Holmes agreed that the way in which Nichol had gone about removing the cross was ill advised, they framed the central issue of the controversy differently. Professor Holmes argued for the removal of the cross on the basis of historical accuracy. Outlining a history of crosses in Christian worship, Holmes contended that it was not until the 1300s that the three-dimensional cross appeared in worship spaces and not until the 1930s that the cross appeared in the Wren Chapel. Moreover, Holmes argued, it was strange that evangelicals such as Newt Gingrich should be among the most vociferous in the debate, given the fact that American evangelicals only recently used crosses in their houses of worship.

D'Souza argued for the reinstatement of the cross on the basis of tolerance rather than historical accuracy. For D'Souza, Professor Holmes's desire to return to the historical condition of the chapel sidestepped what the removal of such a cross meant to a contemporary society no longer united by a shared Christian identity as in eighteenth-century America. He countered Holmes's authenticity position, saying, "President Nichol made a decision which had nothing to do with the original status of this chapel."[8] He argued that if Holmes wanted to go back to the original condition of this chapel, then it followed that the College of William & Mary also needed to go back to its original identity as an Anglican college.

Most important for D'Souza, the removal of the cross was far from an act of religious equality or a move toward ideological neutrality but rather "liberal tolerance doing spade work for secularism." He defined the central choice as whether "the public square [should] be totally secular with Christianity driven out of it, or is tolerance a two-way street in which Christians and non-Christians both have access to a public space."[9] To remove the cross would signal intolerance to Christians in this view.

Writing elsewhere in support of D'Souza's position, Gingrich extended the tolerance argument to its logical conclusion and brought into sharp focus the problem of the chapel building itself in a modern university. Gingrich argued that President Nichol's desire for an end to religious exclusion "would require not just a stripping of the altar, but a shuttering of the chapel." "After all," he concluded, "if the presence of a Cross in the chapel signals that non-Christians are less than full members of the community, then the presence of a chapel on a public campus must similarly signal that non-believers are somehow outsiders."[10] Chapels in colleges and universities are never neutral spaces. Whereas a chapel fit easily within the Anglican identity of William & Mary in the eighteenth century, its meaning in the twenty-first century was uncertain.

As Gingrich's comment reveals, the controversy over the cross at William & Mary was a proxy for an argument over the chapel space itself. No matter what the college decided to do with the object of the cross, the presence of the chapel was problematic for a once-Anglican college turned public institution. The William & Mary chapel distills the lingering questions about religion on campus: How do institutions with a Christian past—and Christian spaces—alter their campuses to reflect identities in which Christianity no longer plays a central role?

How far do colleges and universities have to go to accommodate multiple beliefs and nonbelief? What should you do with a chapel in changed times?

The conclusion of the William & Mary controversy leaves unsatisfying answers to these questions. In a compromise, the cross now resides in a clear acrylic glass box resting on a small table at the side of the chapel. The cross is taken out of the box for Christian services but otherwise put away or even shrouded. The cross is present in the space but apart from it. The William & Mary chapel, like those at Harvard, Princeton, and MIT, is a white elephant, an enduring artifact of a religious past whose role is now both unclear and greatly diminished. While religious activity may have a real and vibrant life in sectarian spaces ringing the campus periphery or in some smaller gatherings on the campus itself, by the late twentieth century religion was removed from a central place in the mission of the modern American university. In the 1927 cartoon about the Princeton University Chapel, the child's question, "Mummy, *is* that thing a white elephant?," seems to now have a clear answer. Religious architecture on the campus has lost its real value in an era when religion, even defined beyond Christianity, no longer plays a central role in the formation and education of the American student.

Introduction

1. *Princeton Tiger* 37, no. 7 (15 December 1927): 34. Emphasis in the original.

2. Among the extensive works on secularization, see, for example, Steve Bruce, ed., *Religion and Modernization: Historians and Sociologists Debate the Seculari-zation Thesis* (Oxford: Clarendon Press, 1992). The religious historian David Hollinger presents an interesting reconsideration of the secularization thesis for the United States and provides an introductory historiography in "The 'Secularization' Question and the United States in the Twentieth Century," *Church History* 70, no. 1 (March 2001): 132–43. See also C. John Sommerville, "Post-secularism Marginalizes the University: A Rejoinder to Hollinger," *Church History* 71, no. 4 (December 2002): 848–57. I am grateful to Jeanne Halgren Kilde for calling my attention to these articles.

3. A number of scholars have examined the historical events that changed the position of religion within higher education. Douglas Sloan explores how such theologians as H. Richard Niebuhr, Reinhold Niebuhr, and Paul Tillich in the mid-twentieth century sought to integrate the truths of knowledge, especially scientific knowledge dominant within higher education, and the truths of faith into a "two-realm theory of truth" in *Faith and Knowledge* (Louisville, KY: Westminster John Knox Press, 1994). Sloan's chapter 1, "The Church, the University, and the Faith-Knowledge Issue: The Background," is a particularly useful starting point for understanding the tensions between religion and modern knowledge. The essays in George Marsden and Bradley J. Longfield, eds., *The Secularization of the Academy* (New York: Oxford University Press, 1992) explore various aspects of secularization in higher education. George Marsden takes up the story of universities' secularization in greater detail in *The Soul of the American University: From Protestant Establishment to Established Nonbelief* (New York: Oxford University Press, 1994), arguing for a benign "methodological secularization," where pious believers distanced faith

from the scientific process, that led to an overt "ideological secularization" in the university. Julie A. Reuben's *The Making of the Modern University: Intellectual Transformation and the Marginalization of Morality* (Chicago: University of Chicago Press, 1996) is largely a response to Marsden, in which she argues that the active failure to modernize religion, rather than a passive methodological secularization, prompted the divide between morality and knowledge. Jon H. Roberts and James Turner's *The Sacred and the Secular University* (Princeton: Princeton University Press, 2000) summarizes the major issues surrounding the rise of science in the university and argues that specialization and inquiry replaced religious perspectives in defining the university mission. James Turner also considers the broader intellectual question of how unbelief even became possible in *Without God, without Creed: The Origins of Unbelief in America* (Baltimore: Johns Hopkins University Press, 1985). For an examination of the history of religion within one institution that traces many of these themes, see P. C. Kemeny, *Princeton in the Nation's Service: Religious Ideals and Educational Practice, 1868–1928* (New York: Oxford University Press, 1998). His chapter 5, "Religion and the Modern American University, 1910–1928," argues that universities preserved religion by transforming it, the same argument I advance here. Conrad Cherry provides a parallel narrative about university divinity schools and their failure to assert a Protestant vision of a Christian America in *Hurrying toward Zion: Universities, Divinity Schools, and American Protestantism* (Bloomington: Indiana University Press, 1995).

4. For arguments and evidence that the secularization thesis has been proven wrong, especially in regard to religious practices on the university campus, see Conrad Cherry, Betty A. De Berg, and Amanda Potterfield, *Religion on Campus* (Chapel Hill: University of North Carolina Press, 2001); and Douglas Jacobsen and Rhonda Hustedt Jacobsen, *No Longer Invisible: Religion in University Education* (New York: Oxford University Press, 2012).

5. For a detailed history of the fate of religious ties in seventeen institutions of various denominations, see James Tunstead Burtchaell, *The Dying of the Light: The Disengagement of Colleges and Universities from Their Christian Churches* (Grand Rapids, MI: Eerdmans, 1998); and the useful review of Burtchaell's book, George M. Marsden, "Dying Lights—Review Essay," *Christian Scholar's Review* 29, no. 1 (February 1999): 177–81.

6. Burtchaell, *The Dying of the Light*, 51–52.

7. Marsden, *The Soul of the American University*, 410.

8. Roberts and Turner, *The Sacred and the Secular University*, 27–31.

9. Sloan, *Faith and Knowledge*, ix.

10. Roberts and Turner, *The Sacred and the Secular University*, 70.

11. In 1913, Columbia University zoologist Henry Fairfield Osborn called natural scientists "the new order of sainthood." Others called science the "new priesthood." As quoted in Sloan, *Faith and Knowledge*, 22.

12. Sloan, *Faith and Knowledge*, 22.

13. The Danforth Chapel program at several American public universities is a notable exception. See Margaret M. Grubiak, "The Danforth Chapel Program on the Public American Campus," *Buildings & Landscapes* 19, no. 2 (Fall 2012): 77–96.

14. Charles H. Brent, letter, n.d. (ca. 1925), UAI 5.160 President's Office, Abbott L. Lowell Papers, series 1922–1925, folder 215, Harvard University Archives, Harvard Library. Courtesy of the Harvard University Archives.

15. Charles Z. Klauder and Herbert C. Wise, *College Architecture in America and Its Part in the Development of the Campus* (New York: Charles Scribner's Sons, 1929), 93.

Chapter 1. The Chapel in the Age of Science

1. S. A. Mitchell, "The Foucault's Pendulum in St. Paul's Chapel," *Columbia University Quarterly* (March 1908): 195–97.

2. John B. Pine to Nicholas Murray Butler, 31 January 1908, Central Files 1.1.742, St. Paul's Chapel, folder 1, Columbia University Archives and Columbiana Library, Columbia University. Pine was the chairman of Columbia's Buildings and Grounds Committee.

3. Nicholas Murray Butler to John B. Pine, 3 February 1908, Central Files 1.1.742, St. Paul's Chapel, folder 1, Columbia University Archives and Columbiana Library, Columbia University.

4. For surveys on the history of higher education in America, see Richard Hofstadter and Walter P. Metzger, *The Development of Academic Freedom in the United States* (New York: Columbia University Press, 1955); Frederick Rudolph, *The American College and University: A History* (New York: Alfred A. Knopf, 1962); Laurence R. Veysey, *The Emergence of the American University* (Chicago: University of Chicago Press, 1965); and John R. Thelin, *A History of American Higher Education* (Baltimore: Johns Hopkins University Press, 2004).

5. For the influence of the German model on American universities, see Veysey, *Emergence of the American University,* 125–33; and George M. Marsden, *The Soul of the American University: From Protestant Establishment to Establish Nonbelief* (New York: Oxford University Press, 1944), 104, 153–54, 183–84.

6. "Carnegie Millions for College Pension Fund," *New York Times,* 28 April 1905, 1.

7. See William F. Buckley Jr., *God and Man at Yale: The Superstitions of "Academic Freedom"* (Chicago: Henry Regnery Company, 1951).

8. George Wilson Pierson, *Yale College: An Educational History, 1871–1921* (New Haven: Yale University Press, 1952), 12–13.

9. See *Princeton Alumni Weekly* 14, no. 23 (18 March 1914): 467–68; see also P. C. Kemeny, *Princeton in the Nation's Service: Religious Ideals and Educational Practice, 1868–1928* (New York: Oxford University Press, 1998), 183.

10. See *Princeton Tiger* 16, no. 2 (October 1905), copy located in AC 144 Dean of Religious Life and Chapel Records, box 13, Princeton University Archives, Seeley G. Mudd Manuscript Library.

11. As quoted in "Assails Yale's Chapel," *New York Times,* 24 January 1926, 7.

12. Former *Yale Daily News* chairman Carlos F. Stoddard said in 1926, "On Sundays the gathering loses whatever religious significance it might hold since the service must not offend any number of faiths. The natural and inevitable result is that while it doesn't offend any faith, neither can it appeal to any faith." As quoted in Ralph Henry Gabriel, *Religion and Learning at Yale: The Church of Christ in the College and University, 1757–1957* (New Haven: Yale University Press, 1958), 227.

13. Sara Margaret Ritchey, *Life of the Spirit, Life of the Mind: Rockefeller Memorial Chapel at 75* (Chicago: University of Chicago Library, 2004), 13.

14. Ralph Adams Cram, "Recent University Architecture in the United States," *Journal of the Royal Institute of British Architects* 101, no. 1903 (25 May 1912): 498.

15. See Alex Duke, *Importing Oxbridge: English Residential Colleges and American Universities* (New Haven: Yale University Press, 1996). Duke is careful to point out that what American educators perceived to be the educational system at Oxford and Cambridge was actually different from the reality, a difference between what Duke terms the perceived and the noumenal past. For a discussion on the whole man theory of education, see in particular chapter 2, "The Whole Man and the Gentleman Scholar," 39–64.

16. Ralph Adams Cram, "The New Boston College," *American Architect* 119, no. 2369 (8 June 1921): 615.

17. For an understanding of liberal Protestantism, I have relied on William Hordern, *A Layman's Guide to Protestant Theology* (New York: Macmillan, 1955); and William R. Hutchinson, *The Modernist Impulse in American Protestantism* (Cambridge, MA: Harvard University Press, 1976). See also Jon H.

Roberts and James Turner, *The Sacred and the Secular University* (Princeton: Princeton University Press, 2000), 67–68. Liberal Protestants are also defined relative to fundamentalists, who took a more literal approach to the Bible and did not seek to reconcile religion with modern thought.

18. George M. Marsden, "The Soul of the American University: A Historical Overview," in *The Secularization of the Academy,* ed. George M. Marsden and Bradley J. Longfield (New York: Oxford University Press, 1992), 22.

19. "Statement of the Rev. Elmore M. McKee, University Chaplain, to the Corporation," 13 December 1930, RU 30, RG 1-B Yale Corporation Records of Committee on Architectural Plan 1913–1931, ACCN 1932-A-007, box 2, folder 22, Manuscripts and Archives, Yale University Library.

20. As quoted in Raymond Knox, "Chapel Plans and Purposes," *Columbia University Quarterly* 10, no. 4 (September 1908): 475.

21. Hibben said in 1925, "Now is not the time to abolish required Sunday chapel. When the new chapel has been erected I should be very glad if it would be possible for the student body enthusiastically to support a voluntary service." As quoted in "Princeton Chapel to Cost $1,500,000," *New York Times,* 31 March 1925, 17.

22. Marsden, *Soul of the American University*, 340.

Chapter 2. The Image of University Religion

1. "Laying the Chapel Cornerstone," *Princeton Alumni Weekly* 25, no. 26 (17 June 1925).

2. See Robert L. Kelly, "Editorial: College Chapel, 1930," and "American College Chapels: The College Chapel," both in *Christian Education* 8, no. 5 (February 1930): 269–321. See also the account of chapel buildings by Charles C. Mierow, "College Chapel Buildings in America," *Association of American Colleges Bulletin* 16, no. 1 (March 1930): 127–44.

3. Alfred L. Aiken, chairman of the Yale Alumni Board, to Carl A. Lohmann, 27 April 1926, RU 164 Records of the Yale Corporation, Group 1-F, series I, box 6, folder 85, Manuscripts and Archives, Yale University Library.

4. Charles Z. Klauder and Herbert C. Wise, *College Architecture in America and Its Part in the Development of the Campus* (New York: Charles Scribner's Sons, 1929), 93.

5. Floyd W. Reeves et al., *University Plant Facilities, University of Chicago Survey*, vol. 9 (Chicago: University of Chicago Press, 1933), 124–25. The most expensive buildings per cubic foot were the university's two chapels, Rockefeller Memorial Chapel and the smaller Joseph Bond Chapel.

6. "Report of the Committee to Visit Appleton Chapel and Phillips Brooks House," ca. 1925, p. 29, UAI 5.160 President's Office, Abbott L. Lowell Papers, series 1922–1925, box 189, folder 192, Harvard University Archives, Harvard Library. Courtesy of the Harvard University Archives.

7. Charles H. Brent, letter, n.d. (ca. 1925), UAI 5.160 President's Office, Abbott L. Lowell Papers, series 1922–1925, folder 215, Harvard University Archives, Harvard Library. Courtesy of the Harvard University Archives.

8. As quoted in "Report of the Committee to Visit Appleton Chapel and Phillips Brooks House," ca. 1925, p. 34, UAI 5.160 President's Office, Abbott L. Lowell Papers, series 1922–1925, folder 192, Harvard University Archives, Harvard Library. Courtesy of the Harvard University Archives.

9. Herbert Parrish, "Religion Goes to College: The New Chapel at Princeton," *Century Magazine* 117 (January 1929): 281–89.

10. For Herbert Parrish's obituary, see "Rev. Dr. Herbert Parrish," *New York Times,* 9 August 1941, 15. Parrish was educated at Trinity College in Hartford, the General Theological Seminary, New York, the University of Pennsylvania, and Johns Hopkins University.

11. Parrish, "Religion Goes to College," 284.

12. These religious reform movements promoted a return to Gothic architecture in parish design and liturgical ceremonies in an effort to reform Anglican worship. The groups imported this message of reform to the United States beginning in the 1840s. For a detailed description of the influence of these groups in America, see Phoebe B. Stanton's foundational *The Gothic Revival & American Church Architecture: An Episode in Taste, 1840–1856* (Baltimore: Johns Hopkins University Press, [1968] 1997).

13. Parrish, "Religion Goes to College," 281–82.

14. Ibid., 283.

15. Ibid.

16. Ibid., 286.

17. For accounts of Princeton's chapel development and the religious and social factors surrounding the construction of the Princeton University Chapel specifically, see Sara E. Bush and P. C. Kemeny, "The Princeton University Chapels: An Architectural and Religious History," *Princeton University Library Chronicle* 60, no. 3 (Spring 1999): 317–52; P. C. Kemeny, *Princeton in the Nation's Service: Religious Ideals and Educational Practice, 1868–1928* (New York: Oxford University Press, 1998), 173–219; and W. Barksdale Maynard, *Princeton: America's Campus* (University Park, PA: Pennsylvania State University Press, 2012), 138–49.

18. Ralph Adams Cram, "College and University Chapels," *Architectural Forum* 44, no. 6 (June 1926): 367.

19. "The Architects' Description of the Chapel Designs," *Princeton Alumni Weekly* 22, no. 8 (23 November 1921): 179.

20. For a detailed account of the process of the Princeton University Chapel's design, as well as a detailed analysis of its stained glass, see Johanna G. Seasonwein, *Princeton and the Gothic Revival, 1870–1930* (Princeton: Princeton University Press, 2012), 100–123.

21. The major works on Ralph Adams Cram remain Robert Muccigrosso, *American Gothic: The Mind and Art of Ralph Adams Cram* (Washington, DC: University Press of America, 1980); Douglass Shand-Tucci, *Ralph Adams Cram: Life and Architecture* (Amherst: University of Massachusetts Press, 1995); and *Ralph Adams Cram: An Architect's Four Quests* (Amherst: University of Massachusetts Press, 2005).

22. Ralph Adams Cram, "Recent University Architecture in the United States," *Journal of the Royal Institute of British Architects* 101, no. 1903 (25 May 1912): 497.

23. Ibid. Cram's reference to the longevity of the English educational ideal is precisely the perceived past of the English educational system that Alex Duke argues differed significantly from the actual past. Alex Duke, *Importing Oxbridge: English Residential Colleges and American Universities* (New Haven: Yale University Press, 1996), 8, 11–38.

24. Woodrow Wilson, "An Address to the Princeton Alumni of New York," 9 December 1902, in *The Papers of Woodrow Wilson*, ed. Arthur S. Link et al. (Princeton: Princeton University Press, 1966–94), 14:269, 271.

25. See "Cambridge and Princeton: A Collection of Pictures Showing the Striking Similarities between Some of Our College Buildings and the Buildings of a Famous English University," *Princeton Alumni Weekly* 25, no. 30 (6 May 1925): 731–35, 737.

26. Charles L. Candee, Class of 1895, Letter to the Editor, "The Proposed New Chapel," *Princeton Alumni Weekly* 22, no. 14 (18 January 1922): 311.

27. Cram and Ferguson, "The Architects' Description of the Chapel Designs," *Princeton Alumni Weekly* 22, no. 8 (23 November 1921): 179.

28. David Coyle, Class of 1908, Letter to the Editor, "A Suggested Compromise," *Princeton Alumni Weekly* 22, no. 24 (29 March 1922): 527.

29. Candee, "The Proposed New Chapel."

30. John A. Clinton Gray, "Princeton's Gothic Chapel: Upon Seeing the Plans for Princeton's Gothic Chapel," *Nassau Literary Magazine* 79, no. 2 (June 1923): 88.

31. Ibid., 91.

32. Ibid., 89.

33. Parrish, "Religion Goes to College," 286.

34. Ibid., 285.

35. Ibid., 286.

36. Julie A. Reuben, *The Making of the Modern University: Intellectual Transformation and the Marginalization of Morality* (Chicago: University of Chicago Press, 1996), 268.

37. James Hayden Tufts, "A University Chapel," *Journal of Religion* 6, no. 5 (September 1926): 455–56.

38. F. Bosley Crowther, "An Undergraduate Looks at the Chapel: Time Will Be Required to Bring Appreciation of Building's Significance to a Campus not Irreligious, but Anti-Sectarian," *Princeton Alumni Weekly* 28, no. 32 (25 May 1928): 990.

39. Parrish, "Religion Goes to College," 288.

40. Ralph Adams Cram, "College and University Chapels," *Architectural Forum* 44, no. 6 (June 1926): 367.

Chapter 3.   Locating Religion on Campus

1. James Rowland Angell to Alfred L. Ripley, 26 December 1930, RU 30, RG 1-B Yale Corporation Records of Committee on Architectural Plan 1913–1931, ACCN 1932-A-007, box 2, folder 22, Manuscripts and Archives, Yale University Library.

2. Frederick Rudolph, *The American College and University: A History* (New York: Alfred A. Knopf, 1962), 274.

3. George M. Marsden, *The Soul of the American University: From Protestant Establishment to Established Nonbelief* (New York: Oxford University Press, 1994), 152.

4. See, for example, Dorothy C. Bass, "Ministry on the Margin: Protestants and Education," in *Between the Times: The Travail of the Protestant Establishment in America, 1900–1960,* ed. William R. Hutchinson (Cambridge: Cambridge University Press, 1989), 50.

5. *Johns Hopkins Alumni Magazine* 3 (June 1915): 299.

6. See D. G. Hart, "Faith and Learning in the Age of the University: The Academic Ministry of Daniel Coit Gilman," in *The Secularization of the Academy,* ed. George Marsden and Bradley Longfield (New York: Oxford University Press, 1992), 107–45.

7. As quoted in Hart, "Faith and Learning," 117.

8. The four other firms competing for the commission for the campus were the Baltimore firm of Baldwin and Pennington; the New York firms of Carrère and Hastings and W. H. Boring; and the Boston firm of Peabody & Stearns.

9. As quoted in clipping, "Plans Accepted for Homewood," Johns Hopkins University MS Coll 137, Series I, box 1, folder "Homewood Campus Printed Material," Ferdinand Hamburger Jr. Archives, The Johns Hopkins University. See also John Martin Hammond, "The New Home of Johns Hopkins University," *Architectural Record* 37, no. 6 (June 1915): 483, 486.

10. Grosvenor Atterbury and Frank Miles Day, Architects of the Advisory Board, letter to Ira Remsen, 23 February 1912, Johns Hopkins University MS Coll 137, Series I, box 1, folder "Homewood Campus," Ferdinand Hamburger Jr. Archives, The Johns Hopkins University. See especially Schedules C and D. Though lack of finances compromised the initial ordering of the campus, the process of reassessing the practical needs of the university reveals that Hopkins's leadership did place a value on the inclusion of a religious structure. In the revised building priorities, the Architectural Advisory Board of Grosvenor Atterbury and Frank Miles Day, of the architectural firm Day and Klauder, originally ranked the chapel ninth of ten buildings "desirable for the near future." However, when trustees president William Keyser and university president Ira Remsen reviewed the advisory board's recommendations, they changed the chapel's ranking from ninth to third and finally to second on the list of future buildings. This ordering process is preserved in pencil markings in the President Remsen papers. See Grosvenor Atterbury to William Keyser, 29 January 1912, with enclosures from Office of Grosvenor Atterbury, 15 January 1912, RG 2 Office of the President, box 151, folder 581, Ferdinand Hamburger Jr. Archives, The Johns Hopkins University. This process of rankings illustrates that the president of the university and the head of the board of trustees valued the importance of having a chapel in the campus design, even if such a chapel was only a future dream.

11. As quoted in Hammond, "The New Home of Johns Hopkins University," 487. John Russell Pope designed a large auditorium building to be constructed across from Gilman Hall, but it was never realized. In the 1960s, the Milton S. Eisenhower Library (Wrenn, Lewis & Jencks, 1962–64) was erected across from Gilman Hall and today serves as the main entrance building to the university.

12. Marsden, *Soul of the American University*, 156.

13. Ibid.

14. As quoted in Marsden, *Soul of the American University*, 157.

15. Abbott Lawrence Lowell to Edward Caldwell Moore, 15 November 1927, UAI 5.160 President's Office, Abbott L. Lowell Papers, series 1925–1928, folder 241, Harvard University Archives, Harvard Library. Reprinted in *Harvard Alumni Bulletin* (8 December 1927): 324. Courtesy of the Harvard University Archives.

16. Excerpt from the Annual Report, 1917–18, as published in Abbott Lawrence Lowell, *At War with Academic Traditions in America* (Cambridge, MA: Harvard University Press, 1934), 276.

17. Edward Bruce Hill, Class of 1874, Letter to the Editor, *Harvard Alumni Bulletin* (22 December 1927): 393; and Murray Nelson, Class of 1891, Letter to the Editor, *Harvard Alumni Bulletin* (22 December 1927): 394. See also "Protest Harvard Chapel," *New York Times,* 14 March 1931, 26.

18. H. U. Brandenstein to Abbott Lawrence Lowell, 10 January 1928, UAI 5.160 Office of the President, Records of Abbott Lawrence Lowell, series 1925–1928, folder 241, Harvard University Archives, Harvard Library. Courtesy of the Harvard University Archives.

19. William R. Westcott, Class of 1892, Letter to the Editor, *Harvard Alumni Bulletin* (22 December 1927): 395. Some alumni countered the need for more worship space, saying that the demand for religion had if anything declined. Several Harvard graduates cited, anecdotally, that in their estimation Sunday services were not well attended save for particular occasions and that a large new chapel was therefore not needed.

20. Not all opposition to the memorial church was on the grounds that religion had no place at Harvard. One Harvard student wrote to the *New York Times* to dispel the appearance that Harvard's undergraduates were "hard-boiled, world-weary and 'pagan.'" He argued that their opposition was instead due to the fact that the money would be better spent on other buildings and that Harvard already had a functional worship space in Appleton Chapel. See Walter S. Anderson Jr., Letter to the Editor, "Religion at Harvard," *New York Times,* 18 March 1931, 24.

21. "Push Harvard Memorial," *New York Times,* 8 January 1928, 21. For a brief history of the decision for a church as the war memorial, see "Committee to Scan Harvard Memorial," *New York Times,* 20 February 1928, 7.

22. Lowell discussed his views on the planning of Harvard in an exchange of letters with W. Cameron Forbes. See W. Cameron Forbes to A. Lawrence Lowell, 12 January 1922, and A. Lawrence Lowell to W. Cameron Forbes, 18 January 1922, UAI. 5.160 Office of the President Records of Abbott

Lawrence Lowell, series 1919–1922, folder 15, Harvard University Archives, Harvard Library. See also A. Lawrence Lowell to Landon P. Marvin, 2 March 1922, UAI. 5.160 Office of the President Records of Abbott Lawrence Lowell, series 1919–1922, folder 15, Harvard University Archives, Harvard Library. Courtesy of the Harvard University Archives.

23. Bainbridge Bunting, with Margaret Henderson Floyd, ed., *Harvard: An Architectural History* (Cambridge, MA: Belknap Press, 1985), 126. Notably, the 1896 Olmsted, Olmsted & Eliot plan for Harvard, which seemed to anticipate Widener or at least a much larger library, called for Appleton Chapel to be torn down and a more monumental structure with central plan and apparent dome put in its place, although the purpose of this new structure was not defined.

24. Paul Venable Turner, *Campus: An American Planning Tradition*, rev. ed. (New York: Architectural History Foundation; Cambridge, MA: MIT Press, [1984] 1990), 209.

25. A. Lawrence Lowell to W. Cameron Forbes, 18 January 1922, UAI. 5.160 Office of the President Records of Abbott Lawrence Lowell, series 1919–1922, folder 15, Harvard University Archives, Harvard Library. Courtesy of the Harvard University Archives.

26. See Bunting and Floyd, *Harvard*, 151–52.

27. Ibid., 46.

28. This positioning of Thayer Hall was so that Memorial Hall (1870–77) could be seen from the Old Yard. See Bunting and Floyd, *Harvard*, 67.

29. Appleton Chapel would still be remembered in Harvard Memorial Church. The latter's choir area, which doubled as the morning worship space, was named Appleton Chapel, and a plaque on the exterior commemorates the previous chapel.

30. Abbott Lawrence Lowell to Edward C. Moore, 5 June 1924, UAI. 5.160 Office of the President Records of Abbott Lawrence Lowell, series 1922–1925, folder 192, Harvard University Archives, Harvard Library. Courtesy of the Harvard University Archives.

31. "Report of the Committee to Visit Appleton Chapel and Phillips Brooks House," 24 February 1925, p. 32, UAI. 5.160 Office of the President Records of Abbott Lawrence Lowell, series 1922–1925, folder 192, Harvard University Archives, Harvard Library. Courtesy of the Harvard University Archives.

32. "The Harvard War Memorial," pamphlet, n.d. (ca. 1927), HUB 1555.2, Memorial Church, mounted clippings, Harvard University Archives, Harvard Library. Courtesy of the Harvard University Archives.

33. George Edgell, dean of Harvard's School of Architecture, wrote that Coolidge would have preferred that the Fogg Museum be torn down in order

to allow a different alignment for the church. See George Edgell to Abbott Lawrence Lowell, 5 April 1928, UAI. 5.160 Office of the President Records of Abbott Lawrence Lowell, series 1925–1928, folder 241, Harvard University Archives, Harvard Library. Courtesy of the Harvard University Archives.

34. Bunting and Floyd, *Harvard*, 158.

35. James Rowland Angell to Alfred L. Ripley, 26 December 1930, RU 30, RG 1-B Yale Corporation Records of Committee on Architectural Plan 1913–1931, ACCN 1932-A-007, box 2, folder 22, Manuscripts and Archives, Yale University Library.

36. The most recent comprehensive, scholarly examination of Yale's campus is the detailed and richly illustrated Vincent Scully, Catherine Lynn, Erik Vogt, and Paul Goldberger, *Yale in New Haven: Architecture and Urbanism* (New Haven: Yale University Press, 2004).

37. Timothy Dwight, *Yale College: Some Thoughts Respecting Its Future* (New Haven: Tuttle, Morehouse and Taylor, 1871), 86. See also Ralph Henry Gabriel, *Religion and Learning at Yale: The Church of Christ in the College and University, 1757–1957* (New Haven: Yale University Press, 1958), 239–40.

38. Timothy Dwight, "Yale College," *New Englander* 30 (1871): 645, as quoted in Erick Vogt, "Cultivating Types: The Rise and Fall of the Brick Row," in Scully et al., *Yale in New Haven*, 54–99. Emphasis in the original.

39. Patrick Pinnell in his guide to Yale University argues that Russell Sturgis, who designed Battell and the residential Durfee and Farnam Halls to either side of the chapel, purposefully created this slightly awkward triumvirate as a reference to the siting of Oxford University's Keble College Chapel and its two adjoining dormitories, designed by the English architect William Butterfield. Pinnell makes the case that since Sturgis was a devotee of John Ruskin, the English art critic who advocated the Victorian Gothic style, he might have been influenced by Butterfield, who also was of the Ruskin camp. See Patrick L. Pinnell, *Yale University: The Campus Guide* (New York: Princeton Architectural Press, 1999), 17–18. The placement of Battell Chapel also comes from a small campus plan made in 1866 by the firm Vaux, Withers, and Company. They recommended putting the chapel in this position because it "offers the advantage of a south entrance with an avenue approach which would appear to have been designed in reference to the building" and because it "would also admit of a public access to the principle entrance from College St., which would not be inferior to the approach from the interior of the quadrangle." See Vaux, Withers, and Company to Noah Porter, 23 July 1866, Group No. 1131 Noah Porter Papers, box 3, folder 79, Manuscripts and Archives, Yale University Library. The location of the chapel here also com-

plemented the siting of Yale's Divinity Quadrangle and its Marquand Chapel across Elm Street.

40. John Russell Pope, *Yale University: A Plan for Its Future Building* (New York: Cheltenham Press, 1919). For a discussion of this plan, see Elizabeth Riorden, "The Campus Plans of John Russell Pope," *Precis* 3 (1991): 78–79; Steven McLeod Bedford, *John Russell Pope: Architect of Empire* (New York: Rizzoli, 1998), 160–63; Pinnell, *Yale University*, 77–79; and Erik Vogt, "A New Yale: The Pope Plan of 1919," in Scully et al., *Yale in New Haven*, 248–61.

41. Pinnell, *Yale University*, 77.

42. Pope, *Yale University: A Plan for Its Future Building,* n.p.

43. Bertram G. Goodhue, Wm. Adams Delano, and Paul P. Cret, memorandum to the Yale Corporation's Committee on Architectural Plan, 7 February 1920, YRG 1-B, RU 30 Yale Corporation Committee on Architectural Plan, Acc. No. 1932-A-007, box 2, folder 23, Manuscripts and Archives, Yale University Library. It is unclear whether the advisory committee suggested the construction of a new chapel or if the Corporation had required that a new chapel be constructed. See also Vogt, "A New Yale," 257–58.

44. Report of Architectural Plan Committee, n.d (ca. 1920), YRG 1-B, RU 30 Yale Corporation Committee on Architecture Plan, Acc. No. 1932-A-007, box 1, folder 4, Manuscripts and Archives, Yale University Library.

45. Ibid.

46. For a discussion of Rogers and his role in the development of the Yale campus, see in particular Aaron Betsky, *James Gamble Rogers and the Architecture of Pragmatism*, American Monograph Series (New York: Architectural History Foundation; Cambridge, MA: MIT Press, 1994), 115–18.

47. Ibid., 117.

48. On Rogers's revised campus plan, see "Yale to Remap Campus on New Landscape Plan," *New York Tribune,* 27 January 1924, 14; and Vogt, "A New Yale," 259–61.

49. For Rogers's series of campus plan drawings, see RU 1, YRG 46-A Yale Architectural Archives, film nos. 2140–44, 3532, and 9748, Manuscripts and Archives, Yale University Library.

50. As quoted in "Testing Voluntary Chapel at Yale," *Literary Digest* 91 (30 October 1926): 31.

51. As quoted in "Ending Compulsory Chapel at Yale," *Literary Digest* 89 (29 May 1926): 32.

52. James Gamble to John Farwell, 2 August 1928, RU 30, RG 1-B Yale Corporation Records of Committee on Architectural Plan 1913–1931, ACCN 1932-A-007, box 2, folder 19, Manuscripts and Archives, Yale University Library.

Chapter 4. New Cathedrals for the Modern University

1. John G. Bowman, *The Cathedral of Learning of the University of Pittsburgh* (Pittsburgh, PA: Eddy Press Corp., 1925), 8.

2. Ibid., 7.

3. The University of Pittsburgh became a state-affiliated institution in 1966.

4. Robert C. Alberts, *Pitt: The Story of the University of Pittsburgh, 1787–1987* (Pittsburgh, PA: University of Pittsburgh Press, 1986), 81.

5. Bowman, *The Cathedral of Learning*, 12.

6. Alberts, *Pitt*, 81.

7. The most complete architectural history of the Cathedral of Learning is Mark McCullough Brown, "The Cathedral of Learning, 1921–1926: A History of an Architectural Design for the University of Pittsburgh" (MA thesis, State University of New York at Binghamton, 1983). A copy of this thesis is located in the University of Pittsburgh University Archives. For a condensed and revised version of the Cathedral's history, see Mark M. Brown, *The Cathedral of Learning: Concept, Design, Construction* (Pittsburgh, PA: University Art Gallery, Henry Clay Frick Fine Arts Building, University of Pittsburgh, 1987).

8. Bowman, *The Cathedral of Learning*, 19.

9. Ibid.

10. Ibid., 10.

11. Ibid., 9.

12. Ibid., 8.

13. Ibid., 9–10.

14. The design for the Commons Room, or Great Hall as it was originally known, underwent many revisions before Klauder and Bowman settled on the Gothic design. See Brown, *The Cathedral of Learning*, 12. To garner further support and funding for the Cathedral of Learning, Bowman persuaded the numerous ethnic groups of Alleghany County to create and pay for nationality classrooms in the Cathedral of Learning as memorials to their art, religion, and cultures (Alberts, *Pitt*, 137). The result was seventeen unique classrooms with elaborate decorations, furniture, murals, and paintings that added to the sense of monumentality and decoration of the Cathedral of Learning as a whole. The classrooms included were German, Italian, Czechoslovakian, Polish, Irish, Lithuanian, Romanian, Hungarian, Swedish, Chinese, Greek, Scottish, Yugoslav, English, French, Norwegian, and Russian. Others have been added since the 1930s, and their construction continues today. See Lucia Curta, "'Imagined Communities' in Showcases: The Nationality Rooms Pro-

gram at the University of Pittsburgh, 1926–1945" (PhD diss., Western Michigan University, 2004); and Alberts, *Pitt*, 134–40.

15. John G. Bowman, *Unofficial Notes* (Pittsburgh: privately printed, 1963), 75–76. As Mark Brown remarks, Bowman wrote the book in his eighties, quite some time after the events he recorded. The questionable reliability of these accounts and the possibility of their embellishment require that this book be viewed with caution in reconstructing the history of the Cathedral of Learning (Brown, *The Cathedral of Learning*, 23). Bowman's *The Cathedral of Learning of the University of Pittsburgh* (1925) is a more reliable contemporary account of the impetus behind the building.

16. Significantly, the cycle *Murals for a Great Hall: Man's Accomplishment in the World* was designed for the Commons Room by D. Owen Stephens and F. Morgan Townsend in 1933. The lancet shape of the murals suggests they were to reside within the architecture of the room. The seven panels of the cycle included one titled *Men's Gods—Fears, Hopes and Ideals*. These studies are believed to be held in a private collection. See Brown, *The Cathedral of Learning*, 21–22.

17. Chancellor John Bowman, 7 [?] September 1924, typescript address, 2/10 Chancellor John G. Bowman Office File, 1921–1945, box 16, folder 128, University of Pittsburgh Archives, Archives Service Center.

18. See John Bowman to Charles Klauder, Letter, 5 August 1925, and Charles Klauder to John Bowman, 4 August 1925, 2/10 Chancellor John G. Bowman Office File, 1921–1945, box 16, folder 131, University of Pittsburgh, Archives Service Center. Robert Alberts states that the name's origin has been ascribed both to a worker in Klauder's office and to a university trustee (Alberts, *Pitt*, 100 n.). For a detailed history on the fund-raising campaign for the Cathedral of Learning, see chapter 6, "The Campaign," in Alberts, *Pitt*, 93–107.

19. Paul Venable Turner, *Campus: An American Planning Tradition*, rev. ed. (New York: Architectural History Foundation; Cambridge, MA: MIT Press, [1984] 1990), 235.

20. Bowman, *The Cathedral of Learning*, 8. Emphasis in the original.

21. As quoted in "Oakland Ministers Approve Chapel Plan," *Pittsburgh Press* (7 October 1929), newspaper clipping in 2/10 Chancellor John G. Bowman Office File, 1921–1945, box 19, folder 143, University of Pittsburgh Archives, Archives Service Center.

22. As quoted in "Heinz Memorial Dedication," *William Penn Points* (December 1938): 7, in 2/10 Chancellor John G. Bowman Office File, 1921–1945, box 19, folder 143, University Archives, University of Pittsburgh.

23. A version of this discussion of Yale's Sterling Memorial Library was originally published as Margaret M. Grubiak, "Reassessing Yale's Cathedral Orgy: The Ecclesiastical Metaphor and the Sterling Memorial Library," *Winterthur Portfolio* 43, no. 2–3 (Summer–Autumn 2009): 159–84.

24. William Harlan Hale, "Yale's Cathedral Orgy," *The Nation* 132, no. 3434 (29 April 1931): 472. Hale, who later became a journalist and the Voice of America during World War II, originally expressed his disdain for Yale's newfound Gothicism in the *Harkness Hoot*, an undergraduate magazine that he cofounded and whose name parodies James Gamble Rogers's neo-Gothic Harkness Memorial Quadrangle. For Hale's first lengthy commentary on Yale's Gothic turn, see Hale, "Art vs. Yale University," *Harkness Hoot* 1, no. 2 (15 November 1930): 17–32. See also Aaron Betsky, *James Gamble Rogers and the Architecture of Pragmatism*, American Monograph Series (New York: Architectural History Foundation; Cambridge, MA: MIT Press, 1994), 58–60; and Vincent Scully, "Modern Architecture at Yale: A Memoir," in Vincent Scully, Catherine Lynn, Erik Vogt, and Paul Goldberger, *Yale in New Haven: Architecture and Urbanism* (New Haven: Yale University, 2004), 295.

25. Hale, "Art vs. Yale University," 21.

26. Hale, "Yale's Cathedral Orgy," 472.

27. James Rowland Angell, "Response for the University," in *Addresses at the Dedication of the Sterling Memorial Library at Yale University on 11 April 1931* (New Haven: Yale University Press, 1931), 20.

28. As quoted in Betsky, *James Gamble Rogers and the Architecture of Pragmatism*, 121.

29. Wilhelm Munthe, "A Norwegian Impression of the Building," *Yale University Library Gazette* 6 (January 1932): 56; and quoted in Thomas Frederick O'Connor, "The Yale University Library, 1865–1931" (thesis, Columbia University, 1984), 552.

30. Munthe, "A Norwegian Impression of the Building," 58. Hugh Ferriss's rendering of Goodhue's early library design highlighted the stack tower literally, depicting a white mass rising out of the darkness of its earthy anchor. For a reproduction of Ferriss's drawing, see Scully et al., *Yale in New Haven*, 274.

31. For Goodhue's entry in the Chicago Tribune Tower competition, see Katherine Solomonson, *The Chicago Tribune Tower Competition: Skyscraper Design and Cultural Change in the 1920s* (New York: Cambridge University Press, 2001), 219–20.

32. For a discussion on the development of university libraries in this "golden age," see Dale Allen Gyure, "The Heart of the University: A History

of the Library as an Architectural Symbol of American Higher Education," *Winterthur Portfolio* 42, no. 2–3 (Summer–Autumn 2008): 118–23.

33. Hale, "Art vs. Yale University," 20.

34. Ibid., 26–27.

35. "The Bookstack Tower," *Yale University Library Gazette* 5, no. 4 (April 1931): 77.

36. Munthe, "A Norwegian Impression of the Building," 58.

37. L. Stanley Jast, "The Yale Book Tower," *Library Journal* 56 (15 June 1931): 541.

38. "A Modernized University Library," *Scientific American* 145 (November 1931): 328.

39. Other scholars also have interpreted these spaces as having ecclesiastical connotations. See Susan Ryan, "The Architecture of James Gamble Rogers at Yale University," *Perspecta* 18 (1982):33.

40. "The Sterling Memorial Library," *Yale University Library Gazette* 5, no. 4 (April 1931): 61. In descriptions of the library's design, the reason given for such an overt ecclesiastical reference was the fact that the library was a memorial to John William Sterling. The entrance hall, "constructed in the form of a great nave with vaulted aisles and clerestoried lighting," "leaves no doubt as to the memorial purpose of the building" (ibid.).

41. "Yale's New Memorial Library Will Rival Harkness' Towers by 1928," *Harvard Crimson* (11 March 1926).

42. Eugene Francis Savage (1883–1978), who received a BFA in 1915 from the American Academy in Rome and an MA from Yale in 1926, was a member of the National Society of Mural Painters, founded by fellow painter, Edwin Howland Blashfield, in 1895. Also called academic muralists, these artists, who commonly trained in Paris and studied in Rome, included complex allegories in their works, which often depicted images of imperial America and imbued institutions with spiritual meaning. Another notable mural, ca. 1934, by Savage also depicts Alma Mater in Columbia University's Butler Library, also designed by James Gamble Rogers. This Alma Mater, however, more closely resembles Athena, a classical style more appropriate to the library's Beaux Arts architecture. For the context of the American mural movement between the 1893 World's Columbian Exposition and World War I, see Leonard N. Amico, *The Mural Decorations of Edwin Howland Blashfield, 1848–1936* (Williamstown, MA: Sterling and Francine Clark Art Institute, 1978). For a biography of Savage, see Peter Hastings Falk, ed., *Who Was Who in American Art: 400 Years of Artists in America*, vol. 111, pt. 2 (Madison, CT: Soundview Press, 1999), 2901; and *Historical Register of Yale University* (New Haven: Yale University, 1939), 465.

43. Angell, "Response for the University," 20.

44. As quoted in "The Mural Decoration by Professor Savage," *Yale University Library Gazette* 7, no. 3 (January 1933): 75. As the architectural historian Aaron Betsky argues, while the library's "storage of knowledge is thus controlled by functional concerns . . . its use is defined by a choreography of acculturation dominated by religious, moral, and social models and decoration" (Betsky, *James Gamble Rogers and the Architecture of Pragmatism*, 124).

45. *Harkness Hoot* 3, no. 2 (December 1932): 3. The *Alma Mater* mural was not without precedent. In Yale's previous library, Chittenden Hall, a Louis Comfort Tiffany stained-glass window (1889–90) also included allegorical representations of the sciences and of religion gathered around the personification of Education.

46. "The Mural Decoration by Professor Savage," *Yale University Library Gazette* 7, no. 3 (January 1933): 76. This hammer and sickle is sometimes interpreted as communist iconography. See Betsky, *James Gamble Rogers and the Architecture of Pragmatism*, 248 n. 81.

47. Betsky, *James Gamble Rogers and the Architecture of Pragmatism*, 122–23.

48. Sally M. Promey, *Painting Religion in Public: John Singer Sargent's Triumph of Religion at the Boston Public Library* (Princeton: Princeton University Press, 1999), 103.

49. James Gamble Rogers, "The Sterling Memorial Library: Notes by the Architect," *Yale University Library Gazette* 3, no. 1 (July 1928): 5.

50. Betsky, *James Gamble Rogers and the Architecture of Pragmatism*, 122.

51. See "The Decoration of the Sterling Memorial Library," *Yale University Library Gazette* 5, no. 4 (April 1931): 80–123. An immense collection of images used as models for decoration in the library can be found in RU 696, RG 46-B, Records Documenting Buildings, Facilities and Grounds, Photos and Pictures of Sterling Memorial Library, series II, boxes 6 and 7, Manuscripts and Archives, Yale University Library. For their origin, see Betsky, *James Gamble Rogers and the Architecture of Pragmatism*, 126.

52. "The Decoration of the Sterling Memorial Library," 82.

53. Ibid., 100–101.

54. Ibid., 89. The quotation comes from William Shakespeare's *Henry VI*, pt. 2, act 4, scene 7.

55. "The Decoration of the Sterling Memorial Library," 83.

56. Ibid., 100.

57. Ibid., 103. Figures on other corbels include a student reading a sad story, a student reading an exciting book, and a student "with radio headphones on, books neglected."

58. Hale, "Yale's Cathedral Orgy," 472.

59. Yale's Gutenberg Bible now resides in the Beinecke Rare Book and Manuscript Library (1963), a modern building by Gordon Bunshaft of Skidmore, Owings and Merrill.

60. Munthe, "A Norwegian Impression of the Building," 56.

61. "The Decoration of the Sterling Memorial Library," 88. Below these images is an inscription in Latin "from the colophon of Johannes Balbus's Catholicon printed in 1460 and attributed to Gutenberg's press." For the images used as a model for the images of Gutenberg, see RU 696, RG 46-B, Records Documenting Buildings, Facilities and Grounds, Photos and Pictures of Sterling Memorial Library, series II, box 6, folder 75, Manuscripts and Archives, Yale University Library.

62. Anson Phelps Stokes to James Gamble Rogers, 5 December 1927, temporary folder III, files of Judith Schiff related to the seventy-fifth anniversary of Sterling Memorial Library, Manuscripts and Archives, Yale University Library.

63. "The Decoration of the Sterling Memorial Library," 98–99. For the images used as a model for the bosses, see RU 696, RG 46-B, Records Documenting Buildings, Facilities and Grounds, Photos and Pictures of Sterling Memorial Library, series II, box 6, folder 75, Manuscripts and Archives, Yale University Library.

64. "A Noble Pile," *Commonweal* 14 (26 August 1931): 393.

65. *Yale Record* 59, no. 2 (22 October 1930): 49.

66. "A Noble Pile," 393.

67. *Yale Record* 13 (21 May 1934): 382.

68. *Yale Record* 59, no. 6 (14 January 1931): 211.

Chapter 5. The Postwar Chapel at MIT

1. "18 Churches Win in Architecture," *New York Times,* 11 April 1956, 33. The National Council of Churches Commission on Architecture selected eighteen churches from seventy-two nominations of specifically Protestant churches, though the inclusion of the MIT Chapel indicates that nondenominational chapels also were considered. All nominated churches were of modern design. The top church design—the only ranked position—went to Christ Evangelical Lutheran Church (1949) in Minneapolis, by Eero Saarinen's father, Eliel Saarinen (1873–1950). The council also selected one other college chapel, the nondenominational Danforth Chapel (ca. 1950) by James M. Hunter

at the Colorado Agricultural and Mechanical College (renamed Colorado State University in 1957).

2. A version of this chapter was originally published as Margaret M. Grubiak, "Educating the Moral Scientist: The Chapels at I. I. T. and M.I.T.," *ARRIS: Journal of the Southeast Chapter of the Society of Architectural Historians* 18 (2007): 1–14.

3. "Our Religious Program, from President Killian's Report to members of the Corporation for the year ending October, 1954," in "Dedication of the Kresge Auditorium and the MIT Chapel, Massachusetts Institute of Technology, May 8, 1955," Massachusetts Institute of Technology, Office of the President, Records of Karl Taylor Compton and James Rhyne Killian, AC 4, box 131, folder 10, Massachusetts Institute of Technology, Institute Archives and Special Collections, Cambridge. Also printed in "President's Report Issue," *Massachusetts Institute of Technology Bulletin* 90, no. 2 (November 1954): 29–32.

4. As quoted in "An Invitation . . . ," n.d. [ca. 1949–50], John T. Rettaliata Papers, Acc. No. 19981.184, box 3, folder 13, University Archives, Paul V. Gavin Library, Illinois Institute of Technology, Chicago.

5. John Corrigan and Winthrop S. Hudson, *Religion in America: An Historical Account of the Development of American Religious Life*, 7th ed. (Upper Saddle River, NJ: Pearson Education, 2004), 385.

6. Ibid., 385 n. 32.

7. Merrimon Cuninggim, *The College Seeks Religion*, Yale Studies in Religious Education, vol. 20 (New Haven: Yale University Press, 1947), 30. Cuninggim conducted a study of religious programs at several universities, including Yale, Princeton, and the University of Chicago. Notably, he cited the chapels at Princeton and the University of Chicago as significant in contributing to the religious programs.

8. See Margaret M. Grubiak, "The Danforth Chapel Program on the Public American Campus," *Buildings & Landscapes* 19, no. 2 (Fall 2012): 77–96.

9. Bosworth's resume recited a thoroughly classical training. After graduating from the MIT architecture department in 1889, Bosworth joined the office of Henry Hobson Richardson and later worked in the office of Frederick Law Olmsted on the design for Stanford University. He also worked with the firm of Carrère and Hastings on the 1901 Pan-American Exposition in Buffalo, and he counted the Rockefellers among his clients. Bosworth also had a substantial European architectural education. As a staff member of the *American Architect*, Bosworth traveled to Europe frequently. He studied in schools in London and at the École des Beaux-Arts in Paris, where he also worked on

the Louvre. For a biography of Bosworth, see "Architect for New Buildings Selected," *Technology Review* 15, no. 3 (March 1913): 157–59. For further background on Bosworth and a history of the development of MIT's Cambridge campus, see Mark Jarzombek, *Designing MIT: Bosworth's New Tech* (Boston: Northeastern University Press, 2004).

10. William Welles Bosworth, "New Group for Massachusetts Institute of Technology, Cambridge, Mass.," *American Architect* 105, no. 2118 (26 July 1916): 50.

11. A 1962 memorandum recounting a conversation with MIT Building Committee chair Robert Kimball states that "the initial idea" for the chapel had been discussed by the Pugh family connected with the Sun Oil Company during the Compton administration. See O. Robert Simha, memorandum "M.I.T. Chapel: Conversation with Robert Kimball," 26 March 1962, Massachusetts Institute of Technology, Planning Office, AC 205, series 4, box 4, folder "MIT—academic real estate—chapel," Massachusetts Institute of Technology, Institute Archives and Special Collections, Cambridge.

12. William Welles Bosworth to Professor Irwin H. Schell, "An outline of the reasoning which has produced the accompanying designs for a Chapel, or Meditation Hall, for the Massachusetts Institute of Technology," 30 November 1938, Massachusetts Institute of Technology, Office of the President, Records of Karl Taylor Compton and James Rhyne Killian, AC 4, box 33, folder 9, Massachusetts Institute of Technology, Institute Archives and Special Collections, Cambridge.

13. Ibid.

14. Ibid.

15. Ibid.

16. Ibid. Bosworth offered more details for the altar that similarly attempted to accommodate both Christian and non-Christian faiths: "On the altar, and lit from below I should place two angels in sculptured glass. They should be kneeling, in an attitude of prayer, on either side of a newborn babe, also sculptured in glass and lit from below. This babe would not necessarily mean the Christchild, but the birth of man—any man—which is the most mysterious, the most inspiring, the most glorious thing we know and the thing which should plunge us into the deepest thought."

17. Francis E. Wylie, *M.I.T. in Perspective: A Pictorial History of the Massachusetts Institute of Technology* (Boston: Little, Brown, 1975),102.

18. Ibid., 115.

19. As quoted in Wylie, *M.I.T. in Perspective*, 121.

20. "Balancing Act," *Time* 65 (31 January 1955): 67.

21. For a full account and transcripts of the event, as well as annotations, see the extraordinarily detailed John Ely Burchard, ed., *Mid-Century: The Social Implications of Scientific Progress* (Cambridge, MA: MIT; New York: John Wiley and Sons, 1950).

22. As quoted in "Balancing Act," 66.

23. As quoted in Burchard, *Mid-Century*, 60–62.

24. "Submitted application to establish at MIT a Kresge School of Human Relations, which would enrich the existing program of technological education by increased emphasis on humanities, social sciences, character building activities, and religion," 11 April 1950, Massachusetts Institute of Technology, Office of the President, Records of Karl Taylor Compton and James Rhyne Killian, AC 4, box 131, folder 12. Massachusetts Institute of Technology, Institute Archives and Special Collections, Cambridge.

25. "Our Religious Program, from President Killian's Report to members of the Corporation for the year ending October, 1954."

26. Ibid.

27. Ibid.

28. Dean of Students William Speer to James R. Killian, 29 July 1954, Massachusetts Institute of Technology, Office of the President, Records of Karl Taylor Compton and James Rhyne Killian, AC 4, box 131, folder 17, Massachusetts Institute of Technology, Institute Archives and Special Collections, Cambridge. Speer specifically wrote this to clarify the statement, "An institute of science may well be an environment especially favorable to deeper spiritual insights." Speer wished to avoid the implication that "MIT believes that science is going to provide something necessary for man's salvation which God has not already supplied in the revelation of himself in Christ."

29. Dean Everett Moore Baker, memorandum "Re: The Need for a Chapel Auditorium," to Dr. James R. Killian, 12 December 1949; and Dean Everett Moore Baker, memorandum to James R. Killian, 9 February 1948, and John H. O'Neill Jr. to James R. Killian, 15 November 1949, all in Massachusetts Institute of Technology, Office of the President, Records of Karl Taylor Compton and James Rhyne Killian, AC 4, box 131, folder 5, Massachusetts Institute of Technology, Institute Archives and Special Collections, Cambridge.

30. O. Robert Simha, memorandum "M.I.T. Chapel: Conversation with Robert Kimball," 26 March 1962.

31. Dean Everett Moore Baker, memorandum "Re: The Need for a Chapel Auditorium," to Dr. James R. Killian, 12 December 1949.

32. Ibid.

33. Peter W. Williams, *Houses of God: Region, Religion, and Architecture in the United States* (Urbana: University of Illinois Press, 1997), 6.

34. "Our Religious Program, from President Killian's Report to members of the Corporation for the year ending October, 1954."

35. O. Robert Simha, memorandum "M.I.T. Chapel: Conversation with Robert Kimball," 26 March 1962.

36. "Submitted application to establish at MIT a Kresge School of Human Relations, which would enrich the existing program of technological education by increased emphasis on humanities, social sciences, character building activities, and religion," 11 April 1950.

37. "Selection of an Architect for the Auditorium-Chapel," Minutes of Meeting of the Building Committee, 10 July and 22 July 1950, Massachusetts Institute of Technology, Office of the President, Records of Karl Taylor Compton and James Rhyne Killian, AC 4, box 39, folder 8, Massachusetts Institute of Technology, Institute Archives and Special Collections, Cambridge.

38. James R. Killian to Netherlands Ambassador E. N. van Kleffens, 1 April 1955, Massachusetts Institute of Technology, Office of the President, Records of Karl Taylor Compton and James Rhyne Killian, AC 4, box 131, folder 8, Massachusetts Institute of Technology, Institute Archives and Special Collections, Cambridge.

39. See "Structures—Spherical and Cylindrical," *Technology Review* 57, no. 8 (June 1955): 391–92; and "Saarinen Challenges the Rectangle," *Architectural Forum* 98, no. 1 (January 1953): 132–33. Hsio Wen Shih also provides an account of Saarinen's plan in "Abstract from Thesis for Bachelor of Architecture" [1953], copy in Massachusetts Institute of Technology, Office of the President, Records of Karl Taylor Compton and James Rhyne Killian, AC 4, box 131, folder 5, Massachusetts Institute of Technology, Institute Archives and Special Collections, Cambridge. See also Hsio Wen Shih, "A Student Center for the Massachusetts Institute of Technology" (Bachelor of Architecture thesis, MIT, 1953).

40. Eero Saarinen's vision for the plaza was never fully realized. The buildings along Massachusetts Avenue that disrupt the direct line of sight from the plaza to the original Bosworth buildings were not demolished; Massachusetts Avenue was never depressed to allow for uninterrupted communication between the plaza and the Rogers Building; and the linear building at the plaza's southern edge was not constructed. However, the plaza's primary elements were achieved. Saarinen's domed Kresge Auditorium and cylindrical

MIT Chapel, together with the later brutalist block of the Stratton Student Center (1965) by MIT architecture professor Eduardo Catalano at the plaza's northern border, formed the nucleus of MIT's religious and social life.

41. "Saarinen Challenges the Rectangle," 133.

42. See "Structures—Spherical and Cylindrical," 391.

43. James R. Killian to R. M. Kimball, 3 October 1950, Massachusetts Institute of Technology, Office of the President, Records of Karl Taylor Compton and James Rhyne Killian, AC 4, box 131, folder 5, Massachusetts Institute of Technology, Institute Archives and Special Collections, Cambridge.

44. As quoted in Aline B. Saarinen, ed., *Eero Saarinen on His Work: A Selection of buildings dated from 1947 to 1964 with statements by the architect*, rev. ed. (New Haven: Yale University Press, 1968), 40.

45. As quoted in "Trend of Affairs," *Technology Review* 57, no. 8 (June 1955): 387.

46. In defending the chapel, President Killian wrote that "it is most important to see the design of the chapel in terms of its relation to the auditorium and its setting" and that "in general, the buildings on the west campus are brick and on a scale that seems appropriate to student living." James R. Killian to John P. Connelly, 22 March 1954, folder 7, Massachusetts Institute of Technology, Office of the President, Records of Karl Taylor Compton and James Rhyne Killian, AC 4, box 131, folder 7, Massachusetts Institute of Technology, Institute Archives and Special Collections, Cambridge. See also Saarinen, *Eero Saarinen on His Work*, 42.

47. James R. Killian to R. M. Kimball, 3 October 1950.

48. Saarinen, *Eero Saarinen on His Work*, 42.

49. Ibid.

50. As quoted in "Dedicate Kresge Auditorium and Chapel," *Technology Review* 57, no. 8 (June 1955): 387–88.

51. Saarinen imitated the brickwork that Aalto had used in the Baker House. R. M. Kimball to James R. Killian, 3 June 1953, Massachusetts Institute of Technology, Office of the President, Records of Karl Taylor Compton and James Rhyne Killian, AC 4, box 131, folder 6, Massachusetts Institute of Technology, Institute Archives and Special Collections, Cambridge.

52. As quoted in Saarinen, *Eero Saarinen on His Work*, 42.

53. Martin E. Marty, "Church Building, U.S.A. Part II: College Chapels," *Your Church* 5, no. 2 (April–May–June 1959): 47. See also the remarks of Paul Tillich, Pietro Belluschi, and others, in "Theology and Architecture," *Architectural Forum* 103, no. 6 (December 1955): 131–37, which refers to the MIT Chapel and the chapels at Brandeis University.

54. One guideline for the chapel design suggested, "Although any religious symbolism in the architecture and design of the chapel should be dominantly Christian, ideally the religious symbolism should be such that the chapel could be used for religious services for men and women of all faiths." "Specifications for Auditorium-Chapel for M.I.T.," 17 July 1950, Massachusetts Institute of Technology, Office of the President, Records of Karl Taylor Compton and James Rhyne Killian, AC 4, box 131, folder 5, Massachusetts Institute of Technology, Institute Archives and Special Collections, Cambridge.

55. Pia Panella, in her master's thesis on the MIT Chapel, points to a number of religious references in the chapel's form, including the correlation of the thirteen arches at the cylindrical base to the thirteen apostles and Bertoia's sculptural screen to a reredos. See Pia Panella, "Eero Saarinen's Massachusetts Institute of Technology Chapel: The Architectural Interpretation of Non-Denominational Space" (Master of Architectural History thesis, University of Virginia, 2005).

56. Theodore Roszak to Francis E. Wylie, 24 November 1955, folder "MIT–Cambridge Campus, Building W15—Chapel—Written Material," MIT General Collection, MIT Museum, Cambridge, MA.

57. Eero Saarinen, "Campus Planning: The Unique World of the University, College Buildings, Buildings Types Study 288," *Architectural Forum* 128, no. 5 (November 1960): 130.

58. E. N. van Kleffens, "The Dedicatory Address," *Technology Review* 57, no. 8 (June 1955): 403, 404.

59. Theodore P. Ferris, "The Affirmation," *Technology Review* 57, no. 8 (June 1955): 406.

60. Ibid.

61. Van Kleffens, "The Dedicatory Address," 404. Emphasis in original.

62. Ferris, "The Affirmation," 406.

63. Van Kleffens, "The Dedicatory Address," 403–4.

Epilogue

1. See, for example, Lisa Miller, "Harvard's Crisis of Faith," *Newsweek* 155, no. 8 (22 February 2010): 42–45.

2. As quoted in Alexandra Cochrane, "Nichol Defends Cross Removal at BOV Meeting," *[College of William & Mary] Flat Hat* (29 November 2006).

3. As quoted in Joshua Pinkerton, "Nichol Announces Changes to Wren Cross Policy," *[College of William & Mary] Flat Hat* (20 December 2006).

4. As quoted in Federick Kunckle, "School's Move toward Inclusion Creates a Rift," *Washington Post,* 26 December 2006, B01.

5. Notably, the first president of the ISI was William F. Buckley Jr., whose classic work *God and Man at Yale* directly called into question the erosion of Christian perspective at Yale.

6. Dinesh D'Souza, *What's So Great about Christianity* (Washington, DC: Regnery, 2007).

7. Holmes's scholarship on the history of the Episcopalian Church brings an expert eye to a core issue of the cross controversy. See David L. Holmes, *A Brief History of the Episcopal Church* (Valley Forge, PA: Trinity Press International, 1993).

8. Author's transcript, "Religion in the Campus: Should the Cross be Reinstated in the Wren Chapel?," 2 February 2007.

9. Ibid. Some of the material in this section was discussed briefly in my "What Should Colleges Do with Their Chapels" (guest blog), *Chronicle of Higher Education,* October 7, 2008.

10. Newt Gingrich and Christopher Levenick, "*Laus Deo*: Crossing the Line at William and Mary," *National Review Online* (31 January 2007).

Letters, Papers, Photographs, and Drawings

Columbia University Archives and Columbiana Library, Columbia University, New York, NY
  Central Files
  General Files
  Minutes of the Columbia College Trustees

Ferdinand Hamburger Jr. Archives, Milton S. Eisenhower Library, The Johns Hopkins University, Baltimore, MD
  Johns Hopkins University (MS Coll 137)
  Office of the President (RG 2)
  "Proposed Buildings"

Harvard University Archives, Harvard University Library, Cambridge, MA
  HUV 53
  Mounted clippings, "Memorial Church" (HUB 1555.2)
  President's Office, Abbott L. Lowell Papers (UAI 5.160)

Institute Archives and Special Collections, Massachusetts Institute of Technology, Cambridge
  MIT Office of the President, 1930–1958 (AC 4)
  MIT Planning Office (AC 205)

Manuscripts and Archives, Sterling Memorial Library, Yale University, New Haven, CT
  Noah Porter Papers (Group No. 1131)
  Photographs of Yale-affiliated individuals maintained by the Office of Public Affairs, Yale University (RU 686)
  Pictures of Dwight Hall, Yale University, ca. 1846–1937 (RU 610)
  Pictures of Sterling Memorial Library, Yale University, 1927–1960 (RU 696)

President's Office, James Rowland Angell Presidential Records, 1921–1937
  (RU 24)
Records of the Yale Corporation (RU 164)
Yale Architectural Archives (RU 1)
Yale Corporation Records of Committee on Architectural Plan 1913–1931
  (RU 30)

Museum Archives, Massachusetts Institute of Technology Museum, Cambridge
  MIT Museum General Collection

Princeton University Archives, Seeley G. Mudd Manuscript Library, Princeton, NJ
  Board of Trustees Minutes and Records
  Dean of Religious Life and Chapel Records (AC 144)
  Historical Photograph Collection, Grounds and Buildings (AC 109)
  Historical Subject Files, Grounds and Buildings (AC 110)
  Office of the President Records (AC 117)
  Oversize Collection

University Archives, Paul V. Gavin Library, Illinois Institute of Technology, Chicago
  Drop file, folder "Chapel, St. Savior (AKA Carr Memorial Chapel)"
  Drop file, images, folder "Chapel, St. Savior"
  IIT Executive Committee Minutes
  John T. Rettaliata Papers, Acc. No. 19981.184

University of Pittsburgh Archives, Archives Service Center, Pittsburgh, PA
  Chancellor John G. Bowman, Office File, 1921–1945 (2/10)
  Historical Picture File
  Plan File
  UA Photograph File

Books and Periodicals

Alberts, Robert C. *Pitt: The Story of the University of Pittsburgh, 1787–1987.*
  Pittsburgh: University of Pittsburgh Press, 1986.
Bedford, Steven McLeod. *John Russell Pope: Architect of Empire.* New York:
  Rizzoli, 1998.

Bergdoll, Barry. *Mastering McKim's Plan: Columbia's First Century on Morningside Heights.* New York: Miriam and Ira D. Wallach Art Gallery, Columbia University in the City of New York, 1997.

Betsky, Aaron. *James Gamble Rogers and the Architecture of Pragmatism.* American Monograph Series. New York: Architectural History Foundation; Cambridge, MA: MIT Press, 1994.

Blaser, Werner. *Mies van der Rohe, IIT Campus, Illinois Institute of Technology, Chicago.* Basel: Birkhäuser, 2002.

Block, Jean F. *The Uses of the Gothic: Planning and Building the Campus of the University of Chicago, 1892–1932.* Chicago: University of Chicago Library, 1983.

Bowman, John G. *The Cathedral of Learning of the University of Pittsburgh.* Pittsburgh, PA: Eddy Press Corp., 1925.

———. *Unofficial Notes.* Pittsburgh, PA: privately printed, 1963.

Brown, Mark M. *The Cathedral of Learning: Concept, Design, Construction.* Pittsburgh, PA: University Art Gallery, Henry Clay Frick Fine Arts Building, University of Pittsburgh, 1987.

Bruce, Steve, ed. *Religion and Modernization: Historians and Sociologists Debate the Secularization Thesis.* Oxford: Clarendon, 1992.

Buckley, William F., Jr. *God and Man at Yale: The Superstitions of Academic Freedom.* Chicago: Regnery, 1951.

Bunting, Bainbridge, with Margaret Henderson Floyd, ed. *Harvard: An Architectural History.* Cambridge, MA: Belknap Press, 1985.

Burchard, John Ely, ed. *Mid-Century: The Social Implications of Scientific Progress.* Cambridge, MA: MIT; New York: John Wiley and Sons, 1950.

Burtchaell, James Tunstead. *The Dying of the Light: The Disengagement of Colleges and Universities from their Christian Churches.* Grand Rapids, MI: Eerdmans, 1998.

Bush, Sara E., and P. C. Kemeny. "The Princeton University Chapels: An Architectural and Religious History." *Princeton University Library Chronicle* 60, no. 3 (Spring 1999): 317–52.

Cherry, Conrad. *Hurrying toward Zion: Universities, Divinity Schools, and American Protestantism.* Bloomington: Indiana University Press, 1995.

Cherry, Conrad, Betty A. De Berg, and Amanda Potterfield. *Religion on Campus.* Chapel Hill: University of North Carolina Press, 2001.

Claflin, Carolyn V., ed. *A Fitting Memorial: The Architecture and Ornament of the Sterling Memorial Library at Yale University.* New Haven: Yale University Library, 2002.

Cox, Harvey. *The Secular City: Secularization and Urbanization in Theological Perspective.* Rev. ed. New York: Macmillan, 1966.

Cram, Ralph Adams. "College and University Chapels." *Architectural Forum* (June 1926): 367–72.

———. "Princeton Architecture." *American Architect* 96, no. 1752 (21 July 1909): 21–30.

———. "Recent University Architecture in the United States." *Journal of the Royal Institute of British Architects* 101, no. 1903 (25 May 1912): 497–518.

Cuninggim, Merrimon. *The College Seeks Religion.* Yale Studies in Religious Education, vol. 20. New Haven: Yale University Press, 1947.

———. *Uneasy Partners: The College and the Church.* Nashville, TN: Abingdon Press, 1994.

Duke, Alex. *Importing Oxbridge: English Residential Colleges and American Universities.* New Haven: Yale University Press, 1996.

Fisher, Galen M., ed. *Religion in the Colleges: The Gist of the Conference on Religion in Universities, Colleges, and Preparatory Schools, Held at Princeton, N. J., February 17 to 19, 1928.* New York: Association Press, 1928.

Gabriel, Ralph Henry. *Religion and Learning at Yale: The Church of Christ in the College and University, 1757–1957.* New Haven: Yale University Press, 1958.

Gilman, Daniel Coit. *The Launching of a University and Other Papers: A Sheaf of Remembrances.* New York: Dodd, Mead, 1906.

Grubiak, Margaret M. "The Danforth Chapel Program on the Public American Campus." *Buildings & Landscapes* 19, no. 2 (Fall 2012): 77–96.

———. "Educating the Moral Scientist: The Chapels at I.I.T. and M.I.T." *ARRIS: Journal of the Southeast Chapter of the Society of Architectural Historians* 18 (2007): 1–14.

———. "Reassessing Yale's Cathedral Orgy: The Ecclesiastical Metaphor and the Sterling Memorial Library." *Winterthur Portfolio* 43, no. 2–3 (Summer–Autumn 2009): 159–84.

Gyure, Dale Allen. "The Heart of the University: A History of the Library as an Architectural Symbol of American Higher Education," *Winterthur Portfolio* 42, no. 2–3 (Summer–Autumn 2008): 118–23.

Hale, William Harlan. "Art vs. Yale University." *Harkness Hoot* (15 November 1930). Reprinted in *American Architect* 139, no. 2591 (January 1931): 24–26, 126, 128, 130.

———. "Yale's Cathedral Orgy." *The Nation* 132, no. 3434 (29 April 1931): 471–72.

Hofstadter, Richard. *Anti-Intellectualism in American Life.* New York: Knopf, 1963.

———. "The 'Secularization' Question and the United States in the Twentieth Century." *Church History* 70, no. 1 (March 2001): 132–43.

Hofstadter, Richard, and Walter P. Metzger. *The Development of Academic Freedom in the United States*. New York: Columbia University Press, 1955.

Hordern, William. *A Laymen's Guide to Protestant Theology*. New York: Macmillan, 1955.

Hutchinson, William R., ed. *Between the Times: The Travail of the Protestant Establishment in America, 1900–1960*. New York: Cambridge University Press, 1989.

———. *The Modernist Impulse in American Protestantism*. Cambridge, MA: Harvard University Press, 1976.

Jacobsen, Douglas, and Rhonda Hustedt Jacobsen. *No Longer Invisible: Religion in University Education*. New York: Oxford University Press, 2012.

Jarzombek, Mark. *Designing MIT: Bosworth's New Tech*. Boston: Northeastern University Press, 2004.

Kelly, Robert L. "Editorial: College Chapel, 1930," and "American College Chapels: The College Chapel." *Christian Education* 8, no. 5 (February 1930): 269–321.

Kemeny, P. C. *Princeton in the Nation's Service: Religious Ideals and Educational Practice, 1868–1928*. Religion in America. New York: Oxford University Press, 1998.

Klauder, Charles Z., and Herbert C. Wise. *College Architecture in America and Its Part in the Development of the Campus*. New York: Charles Scribner's Sons, 1929.

Lanford, Sarah Drummond. "A Gothic Epitome: Ralph Adams Cram as Princeton's Architect." *Princeton University Library Chronicle* 43, no. 3 (Spring 1982): 184–220.

Larson, Jens Fredrick, and Archie MacInnis Palmer. *Architectural Planning of the American College*. New York: McGraw-Hill, 1933.

Lears, T. J. Jackson. *No Place of Grace: Antimodernism and the Transformation of American Culture, 1880–1920*. New York: Pantheon Books, 1991.

Levine, David O. *The American College and the Culture of Aspiration, 1915–1940*. Ithaca, NY: Cornell University Press, 1986.

Livingstone, David N. *Putting Science in Its Place: Geographies of Scientific Knowledge*. Chicago: University of Chicago Press, 2003.

Livingstone, David N., D. G. Hart, and Mark A. Noll, eds. *Evangelicals and Science in Historical Perspective*. Religion in America. New York: Oxford University Press, 1999.

Lowell, Abbott Lawrence. *At War with Academic Traditions in America*. Cambridge, MA: Harvard University Press, 1934.

Marsden, George M., "Dying Lights—Review Essay." *Christian Scholar's Review* 29, no. 1 (February 1999): 177–81.

———. *The Soul of the American University: From Protestant Establishment to Established Nonbelief.* New York: Oxford University Press, 1994.

Marsden, George M., and Bradley J. Longfield, eds. *The Secularization of the Academy.* New York: Oxford University Press, 1992.

Marty, Martin. "Church Building, U. S. A.: Part II, College Chapels." *Your Church* 5, no. 2 (April–May–June 1959): 17–29, 47–50.

Maynard, W. Barksdale. *Princeton: America's Campus.* University Park: Pennsylvania State University Press, 2012.

Mierow, Charles C. "College Chapel Buildings in America." *Association of American Colleges Bulletin* 16, no. 1 (March 1930): 127–44.

Muccigrosso, Robert. *American Gothic: The Mind and Art of Ralph Adams Cram.* Washington, DC: University Press of America, 1980.

Oliver, Richard. *Bertram Grosvenor Goodhue.* New York: Architectural History Foundation; Cambridge, MA: MIT Press, 1983.

Parrish, Herbert. "Religion Goes to College: The New Chapel at Princeton." *Century Magazine* 117 (January 1929): 281–89.

Pierce, Patricia D. *Sparing No Detail: The Drawings of James Gamble Rogers at Yale University, 1913–1935.* New Haven: Yale University Art Gallery, 1982.

Pinnell, Patrick L. *Yale University: The Campus Guide.* New York: Princeton Architectural Press, 1999.

Pope, John Russell. *The Architecture of John Russell Pope.* Vol. 1. New York: William Helburn, 1925.

———. *Yale University: A Plan for Its Future Building.* New York: Cheltenham Press, 1919.

Reardon, Bernard M. G., ed. *Liberal Protestantism.* Stanford: Stanford University Press, 1968.

Reuben, Julie A. *The Making of the Modern University: Intellectual Transformation and the Marginalization of Morality.* Chicago: University of Chicago Press, 1996.

Rhinehart, Raymond P. *Princeton University: The Campus Guide.* New York: Princeton Architectural Press, 1999.

Riorden, Elizabeth. "The Campus Plans of John Russell Pope." *Precis* 3 (1991): 78–79.

Roberts, Jon H., and James Turner. *The Sacred and the Secular University.* Princeton: Princeton University Press, 2000.

Rudolph, Frederick. *The American College and University: A History.* New York: Knopf, 1962.

Ryan, Susan. "The Architecture of James Gamble Rogers at Yale University." *Perspecta* 18 (1982): 25–41.

"Saarinen Challenges the Rectangle." *Architectural Forum* 98, no. 1 (January 1953): 126–33.

Saarinen, Aline B., ed. *Eero Saarinen on His Work: A Selection of Buildings Dated from 1947 to 1964 with Statements by the Architect.* Rev. ed. New Haven: Yale University Press, 1968.

Saarinen, Eero. "Campus Planning: The Unique World of the University, College Buildings, Buildings Types Study 288." *Architectural Forum* 128, no. 5 (November 1960): 123–30.

Seasonwein, Johanna G. *Princeton and the Gothic Revival, 1870–1930.* Princeton: Princeton University Press, 2012.

Scully, Vincent, Catherine Lynn, Erik Vogt, and Paul Goldberger. *Yale in New Haven: Architecture & Urbanism.* New Haven: Yale University Press, 2004.

Shand-Tucci, Douglass. "Does the Tower of the Old North Church Belong in Harvard Yard? Does God?" *Harvard Magazine* (November–December 1982): 44–52.

———. *Harvard University: The Campus Guide.* New York: Princeton Architectural Press, 2001.

———. *Ralph Adams Cram: Life and Architecture.* Amherst: University of Massachusetts Press, 1995.

———. *Ralph Adams Cram: An Architect's Four Quests.* Amherst: University of Massachusetts Press, 2005.

Sloan, Douglas. *Faith and Knowledge: Mainline Protestantism and American Higher Education.* Louisville, KY: Westminster John Knox Press, 1994.

Solomonson, Katherine. *The Chicago Tribune Tower Competition: Skyscraper Design and Cultural Change in the 1920s.* New York: Cambridge University Press, 2001.

Sommerville, C. John. "Post-Secularism Marginalizes the University: A Rejoinder to Hollinger." *Church History* 71, no. 4 (December 2002): 848–57.

Stanton, Phoebe B. *The Gothic Revival & American Church Architecture: An Episode in Taste, 1840–1856.* Baltimore: Johns Hopkins University Press, [1968] 1997.

Starrett, Agnes Lynch. *Through One Hundred and Fifty Years: The University of Pittsburgh.* Pittsburgh, PA: University of Pittsburgh Press, 1937.

Stillwell, Richard. *The Chapel of Princeton University.* Princeton: Princeton University Press, 1971.

Thelin, John R. *A History of American Higher Education.* Baltimore: Johns Hopkins University Press, 2004.

Toker, Franklin. *Pittsburgh: An Urban Portrait*. University Park: Pennsylvania State University Press, 1986.

Turner, James. *Without God, without Creed: The Origins of Unbelief in America*. Baltimore: Johns Hopkins University Press, 1985.

Turner, Paul Venable. *Campus: An American Planning Tradition*. Rev. ed. New York: Architectural History Foundation; Cambridge, MA: MIT Press, 1984; 1990.

Veysey, Laurence R. *The Emergence of the American University*. Chicago: University of Chicago Press, 1965.

Williams, Peter W. *Houses of God: Region, Religion, and Architecture in the United States*. Public Expressions of Religion in America. Chicago: University of Illinois Press, 1997.

Wylie, Francis E. *M.I.T. in Perspective: A Pictorial History of the Massachusetts Institute of Technology*. Boston: Little, Brown, 1975.

Theses and Dissertations

Brown, Mark McCullough. "The Cathedral of Learning 1921–1926: A History of an Architectural Design for the University of Pittsburgh." MA thesis, State University of New York at Binghamton, 1983.

Dibble, Charles. "Architecture, Education and Atmosphere: The Early Years of Princeton University, 1896–1916." Senior thesis, Princeton University, 1974.

Grubiak, Margaret M. "Religion in the Campus: The Sterling Divinity Quadrangle at Yale University." Master of Architectural History thesis, University of Virginia, 2002.

Lanford, Sarah Drummond. "Ralph Adams Cram As College Architect: An Historicist's Approach." Master of Architectural History thesis, University of Virginia, 1981.

McNamara, Denis. "Modern and Medieval: Church Design in the United States, 1920–1945." PhD diss., University of Virginia, 2000.

O'Connor, Thomas Frederick. "The Yale University Library, 1865–1931." Thesis, Columbia University, 1984.

Panella, Pia. "Eero Saarinen's Massachusetts Institute of Technology Chapel: The Architectural Interpretation of Non-Denominational Space." Master of Architectural History thesis, University of Virginia, 2005.

Shih, Hsio Wen. "A Student Center for the Massachusetts Institute of Technology." Bachelor of Architecture thesis, MIT, 1953.

Page numbers in italics refer to figures.

MARGARET M. GRUBIAK

is associate professor of architectural history
at Villanova University.